BROTHERS AND SISTERS

PAUL IN THE LITURGY

FLORENCE MORGAN GILLMAN

Nihil Obstat
Deacon David Keene, PHD
Chancellor
Archdiocese of Chicago
December 15, 2023

Imprimatur
Most Rev. Robert G. Casey
Vicar General
Archdiocese of Chicago
December 15, 2023

The *Nihil Obstat* and *Imprimatur* are declarations that the material is free from doctrinal or moral error, and thus is granted permission to publish in accordance with c. 827. No legal responsibility is assumed by the grant of this permission. No implication is contained herein that those who have granted the *Nihil Obstat* and *Imprimatur* agree with the content, opinions, or statements expressed.

This book is part of the Liturgy and the Bible series.

This book was edited by Michael E. Novak. Víctor R. Pérez was the production editor, Anna Manhart was the designer, and Kari Nicholls was the production artist.

Cover: The arrival of St. Paul at Neapolis © Scala / Art Resource, NY

28 27 26 25 24 1 2 3 4 5

Printed in the United States of America

Library of Congress Control Number: 2024932104

ISBN: 978-1-61671-741-4

LBPAUL

This book is dedicated to my precious grandchildren

Anna Florence Cronin
and
Terence John Cronin

"Rejoice in the Lord always. I shall say it again:
rejoice! Your kindness should be known to all.
The Lord is near. Have no anxiety at all,
but in everything, by prayer and petition,
with thanksgiving, make your requests known
to God. Then the peace of God that surpasses
all understanding will guard your hearts
and minds in Christ Jesus."

(Philippians 4:4–7)

CONTENTS

INTRODUCTION

Getting Started

Some Initial Considerations

The readings proclaimed during Mass and other sacramental liturgies offer glimpses of who Paul was and shape our impressions of him. Even now, some two thousand years since Paul lived, we feel his presence through his words. This book will enrich your appreciation of Paul and offer a sharper lens through which to interpret his words as you hear them in the liturgy.

Paul's epistles not only provide teachings that still pertain to Christians today but also allow insights into the beliefs and practices of the first followers of Christ. Passages from these epistles, also called letters, ground us in our ancient heritage, deeply affecting how we Christians live. We encounter Paul's voice both in the readings proclaimed during Sunday Mass and in the readings chosen for liturgies for baptisms, weddings, and funerals. His voice resonates with people, as evidenced by the frequency with which couples choose for their weddings the reading from 1 Corinthians 12:31—13:8a: "Love is patient, love is kind. . . . It bears all things, believes all things, hopes all things, endures all things. Love never fails."

This short book may be of interest especially to lectors and readers as they consider how to express Paul's voice when they proclaim his words. How should a lector or reader convey Paul's forcefulness, his tenderness, his occasional anger, and even his humor? Key to expressing Paul's emotion is an understanding of his life. While lectors and readers are not called to be voice actors, an understanding of Paul and his writings can ensure a more confident, fruitful, fascinating, and understandable reading. Recently, a lector who has been studying Paul related that, after her proclamation of a Pauline text at daily Mass, a friend commented on her comprehension of the reading. A person who has been immersed in a text can often proclaim it with inflections of familiarity and understanding that others notice.

Paul's Towering Influence and Misunderstood Reputation

Occasionally, lectors and readers might struggle to proclaim passages that contain statements about gender, sexuality, or marriage that the contemporary listener may find objectionable. Sometimes lectors even wish they had not been assigned to read on those days! Even when lectors encounter a reading that they find problematic, it is nevertheless their task to read it well; the readings cannot be edited to suit us. But when readings are known to be culturally or socially disturbing to many listeners, homilists have the duty to explain, with the help of biblical theologians, how audiences in the early Church understood the texts and how we might interpret them today. Assemblies appreciate it when the homilist acknowledges the difficulty of certain readings for contemporary listeners, even when the homily will be based on the other readings of that day.

For many decades, Paul has been called a chauvinist, even a misogynist. He has also been criticized for his lack of concern about the evils of slavery, and he has been castigated for his supposed attitudes on such topics as the subordination of women to men, the need for women to cover their heads and keep silent during worship, the need for women to obey their husbands, and whether it is better to be celibate than to be married. It helps to know that, for many decades, biblical scholarship has better contextualized the many simplistic condemnations of Paul. Of course, he will always be recognized as a male of his culturally patriarchal time, but under close observation, as shall be seen in this book, Paul also provides a refreshing challenge to some of the prevailing attitudes of his time.

Paul's Compelling Character and Powerful Writing

From the start, I must tell you that I consider Paul to be my good friend. He has been an intellectual and spiritual companion during the many decades that I have studied him and taught about him. But I did not begin an academic career in theology intending to focus on Pauline studies; rather, I planned to study medical ethics. A required class in the Pauline epistles, however, changed my mind. Paul's expressive language and instructive theological thought were especially compelling to me. Reading his letters, I heard the voice of a man who lived as Christianity was emerging and who was formulating the explanations of what it means to believe in Jesus; it resonated within me. His passionate, clear writing has deeply affected my life. Paul has been on my mind for a long time, intensely so during the years of writing my doctoral dissertation on chapter 6 of the Letter to the Romans at the Catholic University of Louvain, Belgium.

Major New Testament Sources

Before proceeding to speak about Paul, a word about the New Testament sources the book will draw upon is in order. The oldest documents of the New Testament are Paul's letters, all dated between about AD 50 and 64. They will be our primary sources for Paul. (Even though the four Gospel accounts tell of the life, death, and resurrection of Jesus, they are generally assessed as having been written between about 70 and 90.) Though none of the evangelists mentions Paul in the Gospels, Luke writes a great deal about Paul in the Acts of the Apostles. Acts, considered a sequel to Luke's Gospel account, will be our secondary source for information on Paul's life. The book, which was written some two to three decades after Paul's death (late 60s), continues to address "Theophilus," as does Luke's Gospel account, and what has been "handed . . . down to us" (Luke 1:2). Some have suggested that Luke traveled at times with Paul, as indicated by the "we" passages in Acts (16:10–17; 20:5–15; 21:1–8; 27:1—28:16). Under close analysis, those passages seem more likely to have come from Luke's sources, whoever or whatever those were. Some think Luke was relying upon another's notes or a travel diary.

In sum, as source material, Paul's letters and Luke's Acts must be balanced in the complicated and nuanced ways scholars work with such primary and secondary sources on a subject. For example, a primary source is more likely to offer an accurate memory of an event, while the secondary source often reflects others' interpretations of what they saw or heard. At the same time, others can remind us of the details of what has been experienced. So, although Acts is a secondary source, it is considered an important one.

Christ Believers

The term *Christian* will be used frequently and interchangeably with *Christ believers* or just *believers*. The name *Christian* may have been used pejoratively before 45. Originally, around the year 45, outsiders of the Antioch community likely applied the insulting moniker to believers (Acts 11:26). The word might have been intended to negatively imply they were a group duped by that man called Christ. Yet the word caught on and its derogatory nature was eventually forgotten. Paul never uses the term, although he must have been aware that he and his fellow believers had been given that label.

The Lectionary

Throughout this book, I will refer to the lectionary. The lectionary contains the passages from Scripture proclaimed at Mass. These readings are arranged according to the liturgical year, with its seasons of Advent, Christmas, Lent, Easter, and Ordinary Time. (Ordinary Time is divided into two parts—the time between Christmas and Lent, and the time between Easter and Advent of the following liturgical year.) Throughout these seasons are memorials, feasts, and solemnities. The readings for Sundays are spread out over a cycle of three years: A, B, and C. Each year draws its Gospel readings from a different evangelist: A, Matthew; B, Mark; C, Luke. Readings from John occur especially on the Sundays of the Easter season each year. The weekday readings follow a different pattern and alternate, Year I readings on odd-numbered years and Year II readings on even-numbered years.

In addition to the lectionary, I may also refer to various liturgical books—orders of service that contain the prayers and biblical readings for liturgies of baptism, confirmation, weddings, anointings of the sick, penance, and funerals. The lectionary is the major source and orders of service are the minor ones from which Catholics hear biblical readings. I will refer generally to these texts as liturgical or lectionary readings.[1]

For those who do not have the opportunity to pursue Bible study or do not read the Bible more fully on their own, the liturgical readings heard at Mass provide their primary encounters with Scripture. For that reason, many people have an incomplete knowledge of the Bible, making biblically informed preaching essential for conveying the Bible's vast richness to listeners. Carefully prepared homilies can expand on the readings, give them context, and present various interpretations for listeners. Since there is so much to impart, personal biblical study is, of course, especially enriching. For private enrichment, choose one of the many study Bibles that are available. This type of publication usually has many footnotes and an introduction to each book as well as relevant maps.

1. For additional comments on Paul and the lectionary, see chapter 8.

Chapter 1

Paul's Understanding of the Liturgy

Before proceeding to describe Paul's extraordinary life, I will lay out some of his fundamental theology on Eucharist, baptism, and the Body of Christ. As already noted, Paul was living in the earliest days of the formation of what would become Christianity. The period is usually referred to as the Jesus movement, when Christianity was one of the many sects within Judaism. Paul functioned especially as an explainer and elaborator upon the meaning of the events involving Jesus and his teachings.

To set the stage, imagine Paul in a worship space today: If Paul, a man of the AD first-century Greco-Roman world, came as a time traveler to visit some of our parishes today, especially those with more traditional architecture, he might be disoriented. Large buildings, with benches in rows separated by long aisles, focused toward one end occupied by an elevated sanctuary and altar, as well as side altars with statues, a baptismal font, confessionals, and a tabernacle—all of this might perplex Paul. Even the architecture of newer churches in which the main altar is placed within a semi- or fully circular arrangement of pews and where newer baptismal fonts allow a person to be partially immersed, might require some explanation. Our churches reflect more than twenty centuries of historical, theological, and architectural developments and embellishments, as well as the obvious growth in the number of believers. If Paul were observing us today, he might wonder if, with all the developments and accretions over time, the Church has remained faithful to the Christianity he knew. We might even ask that question of ourselves when we hear the challenge to be true to our origins. Are our beliefs and practices faithful to what Paul experienced in the earliest years among the followers of the resurrected Jesus? Christians in every age must continually discern which developments are from the Spirit. Paul's writings form part of the great biblical mirror against which to test our identity. Fortunately, the Bible lays out our Jewish roots and the story of early Christian life.

Did you ever wonder what it would be like if we didn't have the Bible? Christians would still be that community of believers in Jesus' death and resurrection, as constituted and inspired by the Spirit. We are so enriched, however, to have the text. What a gift that it has survived! The Bible helps form the Church at any time in history. If deviations have crept into practices and teachings, the Bible reflects our identity back to us. A major point to remember is that, theologically speaking, the Church is *semper reformanda,* always reforming and purifying itself to remain true to the essence of our origins. Paul's writings are among the major documents against which our faithfulness is measured. And, while we will not be tracing Church history here, it may be noted that, during numerous reform periods in Christianity, the letters of Paul have been beacons of inspiration as well as battlegrounds over what constitutes fidelity to our identity.

Gathered Together for a Meal

Returning to Paul the time traveler, if Paul were taken to a Mass in a home, no doubt he would more quickly feel himself on familiar territory. The worship service in Paul's early years as a believer, beginning in the mid-30s, was a small, home-based gathering. Occasionally in larger cities such as Rome, a few house church groups met together (1 Corinthians 14:23; Romans 16:23). Yet already by the end of the first century, the growth in the number of converts was becoming so large as to make domestic gatherings crowded in some places. Outdoor spaces or houses renovated to make a large meeting room seem to have been the next stage of development. For

Paul, no matter the space, celebrating the Lord's Supper was essentially the gathering of believers for a Jewish Sabbath meal but infused with the Christian understanding of the Lord's life, death, and resurrection and Jesus' words at the Last Supper.

For Paul, no matter the space, celebrating the Lord's Supper was essentially the gathering of believers for a Jewish Sabbath meal but infused with the Christian understanding of the Lord's life, death, and resurrection and Jesus' words at the Last Supper.

The initial developments in what later came to be called the Mass, stemming from the words and actions of Jesus at the Last Supper, are difficult for historians of the liturgy to assess. Sources earlier than Paul's letters are not available. While Acts gives some information, since it was written late in the first century it may reflect customs followed closer to its time. Also, it should be kept in mind that apparently Paul's communities evolved to celebrate more and more frequently, including on other days of the week as well as the Sabbath. That shift may have been hastened by the joining of Gentile believers to the Jewish movement, an integration that affected the times available to worship and created more crowded conditions. Kosher Sabbath meals that were part of the gathering gradually were reduced to the essential bread and wine.

As we become better acquainted with Paul, we will gain an understanding of the origins of the Mass as well as an appreciation for our roots in Judaism. Such an understanding reminds us that the Judaism that Jesus practiced and observed is foundational to Christianity.

Paul's Eucharistic Theology and the Liturgy

The First Letter to the Corinthians 10—14 is an especially informative section of Paul's epistles regarding his thought on liturgical assemblies. His hitherto lifelong celebration of the traditional Jewish Sabbath meal had been transformed when he learned the words Jesus spoke to those who were with him at his last meal on the night he was betrayed. In 1 Corinthians 11:23–25, Paul hands on that tradition (later referred to as the institution of the Eucharist), the earliest known written account of what Jesus said at the Last Supper:

> For I received from the Lord what I also handed on to you, that the Lord Jesus, on the night he was handed over, took bread, and, after he had given thanks, broke it and said, "This is my body that is for you. Do this in remembrance of me." In the same way also the cup, after supper, saying, "This cup is the new covenant in my blood. Do this, as often as you drink it, in remembrance of me."

By way of interpretation, Paul adds the following verse, "For as often as you eat this bread and drink the cup, you proclaim the death of the Lord until he comes" (1 Corinthians 11:26). These words contain the essential core of the Eucharistic liturgy, both then and now. Paul celebrated the Sabbath meal with all the theological meaning it already had in Judaism; then, as a Christ believer, he understood the meal with a new level of meaning: it attests to the death—and thus the resurrection—of Jesus, whose return is expected.

Who Sits Where and Who Eats First?

Eating a variety of food was normal at a Sabbath meal. While it is uncertain exactly when the Christian groups shifted their focus exclusively to the central action of breaking the bread and drinking from the cup, it is clear that consuming other foods at the liturgical meal was problematic early on.

The earliest liturgies might have been similar to the contemporary potluck meal. The strict dietary laws that the Jewish Christians abided by, however, would rule out their eating the non-kosher foods that some brought to the gathering. Gentiles, for example, may have brought pork or shellfish and meat that had first been offered to pagan deities—all unacceptable for Jews to eat. Paul did not, however, solve food dilemmas simply by separating the Jewish and Gentile Christians from each other during the meal. He probably knew that a two-part setup would result in a two-tier community with one or the other group inevitably assuming superiority to the other. In fact, Paul once challenged Peter and Barnabas for regularly eating with Gentiles but withdrawing from them when Jewish Christians with a more rigid mindset about integrating with Gentiles visited (Galatians 2:11–14). From 1 Corinthians (11:17–22; 33–34), it is obvious that other food-related issues arose in Paul's churches, such as who ate first and who got the best food. Paul resolved these matters by telling the Corinthians to eat at home and then come to celebrate the Eucharist. It appears that after this incident in Corinth, the celebration of the Eucharist there centered on the bread and wine. This is an example of how Paul learned from experience and adapted.

Paul's Theology of the Body of Christ

A major dimension of Paul's thought on the Eucharist concerns how believers, by their participation, become united to both Christ and each other. In 1 Corinthians 10:16–17, Paul writes:

> The cup of blessing that we bless, is it not a participation in the blood of Christ? The bread that we break, is it not a participation in the body of Christ? Because the loaf of bread is one, we, though many, are one body, for we all partake of the one loaf.

Developing this theology of the Body of Christ in more detail in 1 Corinthians 12:12–31, Paul points out that Christ believers become incorporated into the Body of Christ through their baptism. Theologians speak of Christ as being a corporate person, meaning Christ embodies all those who believe in him. In this passage, Paul uses the analogy of a body having many parts to underscore how the members of Christ's Body function in a myriad of ways through various roles. For Paul, the human body is not to be disdained as if it were a mere flimsy cage for a person's spirit or soul; he sees the human body as the means of

Paul uses the analogy of a body having many parts to underscore how the members of Christ's Body function in a myriad of ways through various roles.

one's service to the Body of Christ, no matter the significance of the person's role in the Christian community.

In 1 Corinthians 14, Paul outlines the various spiritual gifts that serve to build up the Body of Christ, such as prophesying, speaking in tongues, and interpreting those utterances. While those particular spiritual experiences may be rare in today's parishes, the contemporary assembly takes on a wide variety of roles, ministries, and tasks that enable the vibrant celebration of the liturgy and that contribute to strengthening the community. While the proclamation of Scripture and celebration of Eucharist are at the core of the liturgy, the full array of gifts, even those that may seem peripheral, is required from members of the community. A case in point could be seen in the COVID-19 pandemic. As in Paul's time, with circumstances in flux, the community was able to continue to participate in the liturgy thanks to the expertise, creativity, and contributions of many: the technicians who broadcast and live-streamed Masses; the crews who repeatedly set up and took down furnishings for outdoor Masses; the ushers who guided the assembly members to maintain safe distances, and the other ministers who enabled the celebration of the liturgy.

Paul's Baptismal Theology and the Liturgy

The early Church, including Paul and his companions, appears to have been influenced by the practice of John the Baptist's baptizing in the Jordan River and the memory of Jesus' baptism. Paul and others recognized Jesus in John the Baptist's prediction as "the one who is more powerful than I [and] is coming after me" (Mark 1:7). Just as baptism was a turning point for Jesus to begin his public ministry, early Christians administered baptism to impart a new identity. The Christ believers, however, drew a distinction between the baptism of John, which was a repeatable form of repentance, and their baptism with water and the Spirit that occurred once. Natural water sources—such as rivers, streams, lakes, and the seashore—seem to have been the preferred locations for baptism.

Paul was baptized in Damascus by Ananias (Acts 9:18), although the exact location is unknown. The conversion of Lydia and some other women by Paul took place by a river (probably the river Crenides) in Philippi, where he first met and converted them (Acts 16:11–15). Since Lydia and her whole household were said to have been baptized, it might be assumed that infants were included. That interpretation, however, could be presumptuous as infants, children, and slaves were often disregarded in the reporting of many events. Nevertheless, later explanations of the origins of the practice of infant baptism often cite Paul's conversion of whole households.

Today, near the archaeological excavations of ancient Philippi is a modern church commemorating the baptism of Lydia, who is honored as the first convert in Europe. The church is a circular building with a font in the center for infant baptisms. Surrounding the font are dressing rooms for adults baptized in the Crenides River, flowing just outside. At the site too is a cross-shaped immersion baptistery like those preserved in some ancient churches. In one place, the many forms of baptism Christianity has practiced are brought together.

Baptism, Death, and Life

Every year during the Liturgy of the Word at the Easter Vigil, we hear Paul's theology of baptism during the proclamation of Romans 6:3–11. Two millennia after Paul's address to the Romans, these words still shape our understanding of what it means to affirm a Christian identity:

> Are you unaware that we who were baptized into Christ Jesus were baptized into his death? We were indeed buried with him through baptism into death, so that, just as Christ was raised from the dead by the glory of the Father, we too might live in newness of life. For if we have grown into union with him through a death like his, we shall also be united with him in the resurrection. We know that our old self was crucified with him, so that our sinful body might be done away with, that we might no longer be in slavery to sin. For a dead person has been

absolved from sin. If, then, we have died with Christ, we believe that we shall also live with him. We know that Christ, raised from the dead, dies no more; death no longer has power over him. As to his death, he died to sin once and for all; as to his life, he lives for God. Consequently, you too must think of yourselves as being dead to sin and living for God in Christ Jesus.

After the baptism of the elect at the Vigil, members of the assembly renew their baptismal promises while holding a lit candle. The promises echo the meaning of Paul's words. Christians choose to reject evil and to affirm belief in the Father, Son, and Holy Spirit. The wording in the renewal of baptismal promises effectively conveys Paul's theology that believers baptized into Christ have "died to sin" (6:2) so that they might "walk in newness of life" (6:4). Paul describes a believer's life as one of dying to sin and rising to new life in the baptismal moment. The metaphor implies a death to our "old self" (6:6), which takes place like a drowning in cold, dark, turbulent waters that is followed by surfacing from the dangerous deep, and rising to newness of life.

The Easter Vigil, with its adult baptisms and renewal of baptismal promises, places baptism at the center of Christian life. The influence of Paul is thus vividly felt. And yet, since the Catholic tradition widely and joyfully has long practiced infant baptism, many Catholics may not remember the pouring of water, the renunciation of sin, the profession of faith, or the presentation of the lighted candle. As mentioned earlier, Paul was said to have baptized whole households, such as that of his convert Lydia in Philippi (Acts 16:14–15). Perhaps he included infants when a whole family was baptized. Did he think those infants, once grown, would be faithful Christians? We have nothing written by him about that. We know that he was conscious of children and invoked them in his imagery, commenting, for example, that "those who are led by the Spirit of God are children of God" (Romans 8:14).

Meet at Night on the Bridge . . .

Late in life, Paul would spend numerous years in Rome, some as a prisoner and some as a free person. Foreigners such as Paul congregated in the region of Trastevere, a section of the city on the west side of the Tiber River. To this day, the ancient Ponte Fabricio, a first-century BC bridge over the Tiber, connects the city proper to Trastevere. Standing on it, especially late in the evening, one can envision Paul and those to be baptized gathered on the bridge and then climbing down the steep side hills. Below, along the river's muddy edges, these individuals entered swirling rapids, a truly symbolic act of plunging into death. It would have been dangerous to be baptized here in the night, but the darkness was a cover for a ritual that presented other dangers if performed in the light of day. Imagining the context, one can feel the power of Paul's foreboding imagery of death by drowning. But then, moving into the lights of Trastevere, as the newly baptized would have done, there would be the sense of having undergone a radical death to sin to return to a new life in Christ among the living. The newly baptized would join the full gathering of the group of believers to share in the celebration of the Eucharist.

More recent architecture for baptismal fonts, in both new and renovated churches, has been inspired by Paul's thought and by the need to enable the symbolic power of baptism to be the foundation of a believer's life. The newer structures, often with steps on each side, have returned us to the earliest Christian practice of (full or partial) bodily immersion in water. Immersion communicates a stronger symbolism of going down into a watery grave, dying to our "old self," than does the mere pouring of a few drops of water on the forehead. While circumstances (such as sickness) may at times prevent baptism by immersion, many parishes have embraced immersion as the stronger symbol.

In a similar vein, I once attended the Holy Saturday service in the magnificent medieval Gothic cathedral in Cologne, Germany. It was especially cold along the Rhine River that year and there was no interior heat where my two friends and I sat. Without artificial light, the cathedral felt like a dark, damp, and foreboding tomb. Yet, huddled closely together in anticipation of renewing our baptismal promises, we were like tiny drops of humanity; the lit candles in our hands, symbols both of our rejection of the powers of darkness and our hope for newness of life in the resurrection. The Body of Christ is vibrantly knit and renewed over the centuries. It is always our choice to affirm our fidelity and strive to be numbered among the multitude of Christians. There is great power in the symbolism of dying and rising that Paul bequeathed to us.

How Is the Body of Christ Constituted?

While Romans 6:1–11 is Paul's longest passage on baptism, elsewhere in his letters we can glean further thoughts. In 1 Corinthians 12:12–13, Paul observes: "As a body is one though it has many parts, and all the parts of the body, though many, are one body, so also Christ. For in one Spirit we were all baptized into one body, whether Jews or Greeks, slaves or free persons, and we were all given to drink of one Spirit." This statement complements the focus on the individual in the Romans 6 text with our personal choice to die and rise. Here, Paul focuses also on the result, that the Spirit thus leads each person into a community, the one Body of Christ. From then on, "There is neither Jew nor Greek, there is neither slave nor free person, there is not male and female; for you are all one in Christ Jesus" (Galatians 3:28).

The Imagery of Family

A number of letters in the New Testament, as well as accounts in Acts, reflect the bond among believers as they call each other "brothers and sisters." Paul often uses the Greek terms *adelphoi*—a masculine plural noun that can be translated literally as "brothers"—and *adelph*, grammatically a vocative, as forms of address. Since Greek masculine plurals may include both men and women, as in English, and because we also know Paul normally sent his letters to whole church groups, many modern inclusive-language Bible translations render that term as "brothers and sisters." Further, today the greeting to "brothers and sisters" begins the readings in the lectionary, since these readings are addressed most often to parish assemblies of both males and females.

When a lectionary reading comprises only a small section of a letter of Paul (referred to as a *pericopē,* in Greek, meaning a cutting), the editors have often taken the liberty of inserting "Brothers and sisters" at the beginning of the *pericopē.* This practice is known as adding an *incipit*—the introductory or opening words of the text. The title of this book mirrors that incipit, drawing upon Paul's phrasing to reflect that while he was a person in a patriarchally organized world, nevertheless all his listeners mattered to him. This incipit provides today's lector a reminder that Paul's intention was to address everyone present in the assembly. Pausing to let the eyes take in the assembly before beginning to proclaim the reading might help one communicate Paul's inclusivity.

It may also be noted that the very practice of reading from Paul's letters at a Eucharistic celebration (along with those biblical texts normally read at Sabbath meals) is reflected in Paul's directives. For example, in 1 Thessalonians 5:26–27, he closes with these words: "Greet all the brothers [and sisters] with a holy kiss. I adjure you by the Lord that this letter be read to all the brothers." This implies that the reading was to be done when the community gathered.

The reading from an epistle to a whole group must have determined which of Paul's letters or parts of his longer ones became best known among the believers. What was not read liturgically would likely have remained unknown to those who could not read. Even now, believers who learn the content of Paul's epistles only from what is read at Mass will not be exposed to the fullness of what he wrote, as the *Lectionary for Mass* does not contain the entirety of Paul's writings recorded in the Bible. The same holds true for other books of the

Bible. The *Lectionary for Mass* gives a hearty but still incomplete selection of readings from the Bible.

Paul has helped shape the liturgy we celebrate in one other way. The quotation from 1 Thessalonians refers to believers giving a "holy kiss" as a greeting. Elsewhere, Paul also mentions a holy kiss (1 Corinthians 16:20; 2 Corinthians 13:12). This tradition is continued in what is called the "kiss" or sign of peace.

For Paul, baptism into the Body of Christ—becoming a child of God and a full participant in the Eucharist—was the identity marker of a believer that also served as an equalizer among all persons in the Body. Paul expresses racial, sexual, and socioeconomic egalitarianism in Galatians 3:27–28: "For all of you who were baptized into Christ have clothed yourselves with Christ. There is neither Jew nor Greek, there is neither slave nor free person, there is not male and female; for you are all one in Christ Jesus."

CHAPTER 2

Meeting Paul: His Background and Personality

Paul's life in the eastern Mediterranean regions of the first century was that of a traveler long before he received the life-changing revelation of the resurrected Christ that led to decades of missionary adventures. He was born roughly around the same time as Jesus[1] in the small, vibrant city of Tarsus in the Roman province of Cilicia (now south-central Turkey). The city was about twelve miles inland from the Mediterranean Sea on the Cydnus River. Capital of the Roman province of Cilicia, Tarsus dates back some four thousand years. In Paul's day, it was famed as the place where less than a half century earlier Cleopatra had first met Mark Antony. It was also an important intellectual center. Paul's excellent command of Greek and his knowledge of Greco-Roman literature and culture, apparent in his writings, reflect the ways he benefited from the educational opportunities in that place. Enthusiastic about his geographic origins, Paul described himself as "a citizen of no mean city" (Acts 21:39).

A Hebrew Born of Hebrews

Paul was proud of his roots in an observant family. Once, defending himself against some detractors, he described his thoroughly Jewish pedigree as "circumcised on the eighth day, of the race of Israel, of the tribe of Benjamin, a Hebrew of Hebrew parentage, in observance of the law a Pharisee" (Philippians 3:5). Paul spoke his ancestral

1. The birth of Jesus is assessed as being about 4 BC since, according to Matthew 2:19, Jesus had been born shortly before Herod the Great's death, which can be dated to that year.

language of Aramaic (then the main language of Judea), along with Greek, and read the Scriptures that he was able to quote in both Greek and Hebrew. Since his family resolutely held to their identity, they had probably emigrated from Judea to Tarsus only a generation or two before his birth. Paul's given name Saul recalls his famous Benjaminite ancestor King Saul. The Romanized name Paul reflects the diversity in which he was rooted. In today's world, to be at home in such multiculturalism is greatly valued; likewise, Paul's linguistic abilities and cultural competencies were to serve the early Church in extraordinary ways.

Paul's given name "Saul" recalls his famous Benjaminite ancestor King Saul.

Since Acts 18:3 notes that Paul was a tentmaker, some scholars have supposed that he learned the trade from his family. That his family made their livelihood through tent-making can only be presumed; Paul could have learned the trade elsewhere. Producing a much-in-demand product, Paul easily could earn a living during his travels. One can envision that he made many missionary contacts in the tent workshops as he wrestled long hours to lash together the heavy pieces of material.

The Years Spent at the Feet of Gamaliel

During his formative years, perhaps as a young teenager, Paul was sent to Jerusalem to study under the famous Pharisee, Gamaliel. (Some of Paul's family members may have lived in Jerusalem, since Acts 23:16 notes that in later years Paul had a sister in Jerusalem whose son once warned him of an ambush.) To send the young Paul so far away was already to steer him toward a life of diverse travel experiences. One could make the more than five-hundred-mile journey from Tarsus to Jerusalem either inland or overland down the Mediterranean seaboard; alternatively, the trip could be shortened by taking a series of commercial boats, hopping from port to port. If Paul had arrived by boat, he would have docked in the bustling port of Caesarea Maritima,[2] newly built about four decades earlier under Herod the Great. It seems poignant now that Paul began his young adult life in Judea from that place, since later in life he was imprisoned for a few years in that city.

Any route Paul traveled as a young man would have been fraught with danger, either from thieves or inclement weather. His family must have greatly valued the education they were sending him to experience. Or perhaps it was by his own insistence that he went to Jerusalem to delve more deeply into his Jewish identity. It is interesting to muse about Paul in this period. During his defense before the Jews in Jerusalem, Paul attests to the zeal with which he approached his studies. "At the feet of Gamaliel I was educated strictly in our ancestral law and was zealous for God, just as all of you are today" (Acts 22:3).

Gamaliel is renowned even apart from the references to him in the New Testament. The son of Simeon ben Hillel, and grandson of Hillel the Elder, Gamaliel was a leader in the Sanhedrin, the council of Jewish elders comprised of Pharisees and Sadducees. Paul's education was his culture's equivalent to receiving an advanced degree today.

How might we envision Paul and Gamaliel interacting? One clue is to recall the story of the twelve-year-old Jesus who sat amid teachers in the temple courtyard listening to them and asking them questions (Luke 2:46). That scene portrays the usual way that Pharisees taught their student disciples (all males as far as the evidence shows). The extensive plaza, partly surrounded by beautiful colonnaded walkways, may have been dotted with a few such groups, perhaps with some competitive rivalry over which Pharisee was their mentor. Graduation for these students would occur when the master teacher told a student to sit elsewhere in the plaza and gather his own listeners.

2. Caesarea has been and continues to be extensively excavated. It offers us a significant window into shipping and ports of Paul's times. He passed through this port many times in his life.

The Role of a Pharisee: "You are the teacher of Israel" (John 3:10)

The path to becoming a Pharisee was one of serious study. The position carried authority and respect, but it was not a lucrative position, unlike that of the priesthood of the temple and the positions open to members of allied aristocratic families. The high priest, his predecessors and probable successors, and their aristocratic counterparts, the Sadducees, lived well, as the archaeological record of their known housing area in Jerusalem demonstrates. While priests learned rites, sacrificial incantations, and ceremonial prayers and observances, the Pharisees were educated to thoroughly understand the sacred texts and implement the law of Moses in daily life. They were teachers of all the people, even the poorest. They preserved the Jewish faith and admonished the people to remain faithful to the covenant with God. For Paul to be both a nonaristocratic tentmaker and an intellectual Pharisee made perfect sense in his time. He was to be a teacher of all and to earn his living simultaneously. His total dedication energized him. Looking back on his life in those years before he encountered Christ, he said that he had "progressed in Judaism beyond many of my contemporaries among my race, since I was even more a zealot for my ancestral traditions" (Galatians 1:14).

What were Paul's plans for his future after his years of study when he finally became Gamaliel's younger colleague? Having completed the finest education available in Jewish law, belief, and traditions, and also with a solid trade that could be practiced anywhere, where was Paul going next? Back to Tarsus? Or was he staying in Jerusalem? These speculations raise the questions of how rooted he had become in Jerusalem and whether by that time he had a wife and family.

"The right to take along a Christian wife" (1 Corinthians 9:5)

Paul's marital status has been a matter of much speculation.[3] In his time, marriage was expected of a young Jewish man; it was necessary if a man was to obey God's command in Genesis 1:28 to increase and multiply. Further, to be considered a mature teacher one would need to be a settled, married person. While later in his life Paul appears to be single, it is uncertain that he had always been so. A relevant statement he made in 1 Corinthians in those later years is intriguing. Overshadowed then by concerns that the second coming of Jesus would occur at any time, Paul cautiously advised, "Now to the unmarried and to widows, I say: It is a good thing for them to remain as they are, as I do, but if they cannot exercise self-control they should marry, for it is better to marry than to be on fire" (1 Corinthians 7:8–9). Paul's point was that one should concentrate on spiritual preparation for the imminent return of the Lord, at least as far as possible. Which of the single statuses Paul mentions was his—unmarried or widowed? Neither Acts nor Paul's letters answers that question. It is known, however, that Paul looked positively on marriage. Within these same comments to the Corinthians, who had reported that they were sympathetic to the controversial, exaggerated ascetic position that "It is a good thing for a man not to touch a woman," Paul counterargued in defense of the normalcy of marriage (1 Corinthians 7:1–7).

Later in that letter (1 Corinthians 9:3–5), responding to challenges to his apostleship by other missionaries, and their apparent suggestion that he deserved lesser privileges or accommodations, Paul asserted some of his rights: "My defense against those who would pass judgment on me is this. Do we not have the right to eat and drink?

3. See especially Raymond F. Collins, *Accompanied by a Believing Wife: Ministry and Celibacy in the Earliest Christian Communities* (Collegeville, MN: Liturgical Press, 2013), 111–138.

Do we not have the right to take along a Christian[4] wife, as do the rest of the apostles, and the brothers of the Lord, and Cephas?"

Taking into account what Paul says about marriage, it appears that after his conversion Paul was single, whether a widow or having never married, but passionate about defending his right to bring a wife with him and about being treated with the same hospitality that others were receiving.

"A voice of one crying out in the desert . . ." (Mark 1:3)

If Paul were debating whether to stay in or leave Jerusalem, his decision may have been affected by events unfolding in the late 20s and early 30s. Around 27, rumors were afloat about a man named John, a prophetic figure from Galilee, later dubbed the Baptist. He was drawing crowds across the Jordan River in the northeast with his urgent message concerning the imminence of the promised messiah. Apart from the priests in the temple and the Sadducees, who for reasons of maintaining their power and prestige tended to cooperate with the occupying Romans, many sectors of Judaism were then intensely apocalyptic; they were desperately hoping God would send a messiah to lead in liberating them from Roman domination.

John would baptize his listeners who professed repentance to prepare themselves for the advent of that messiah. In fearlessly speaking out against immorality, however, John enraged Herodias, the wife of the Tetrarch Herod Antipas, the Herodian ruler of Galilee and Peraea. After John publicly castigated Herodias for her incestuous marriage to her divorced husband's brother, she plotted with her daughter Salome and tricked her husband into ordering the beheading of John (Mark 6:17–29). Herodias' victory over the man she may have deemed as just a scruffy protester crying in the desert was

4. *The New American Bible*, revised edition, translation uses *Christian* here to translate Paul's term *adelphē*, meaning a sister who is a fellow believer. Paul is not known to have used the term *Christian*.

hollow, for John had fulfilled his mission: he had completed his prophetic witness for the crowds, attesting that Jesus was the awaited One, sent by God (Mark 1:2–8).[5]

"My house shall be called a house of prayer for all peoples . . ." (Mark 11:17)

Rumors about the death of John and the reports of Jesus' preaching in Galilee likely had reached the circles in which Paul moved in Jerusalem. One suspects Paul may have offhandedly dismissed the significance of such information as just more disruptive behavior from often-scorned Galileans in the north, a people living close to Gentile territory and assumed to be less faithful as Jews. Was Paul shocked to learn that Jesus and some of his followers had since come to Jerusalem, entered the temple precincts, and created a ruckus by overturning the moneychangers' tables? Had Paul heard the message correctly, that Jesus had condemned the current temple system, saying that the temple was supposed to be a house of prayer for all peoples and had been turned into a den of thieves (Mark 11:15–19)? Jesus' obvious critique of the high priests and their entourage could not have been clearer. While Paul may have had plenty of criticism about corruption within the priesthood, the Sadducees, and even within his own caste of Pharisees, an assault on the temple would have shocked him.

"The chief priests and the entire Sanhedrin kept trying to obtain testimony against Jesus in order to put him to death . . ." (Mark 14:55)

Paul would have learned that the disruptive Jesus had been rounded up by the temple guards, brought before the high priest, all the chief priests, elders, and scribes (Mark 14:53) in a mock trial, and charged

5. See Florence Morgan Gillman, *Herodias: At Home in That Fox's Den* (Collegeville, MN: Liturgical Press, 2003).

with blasphemy. According to Jewish law, blasphemy was a capital offense, punishable by stoning. The true reasons for their opposition to Jesus, however, more likely had to do with the power and sense of authority he had demonstrated in his healing and preaching and his castigation of the hypocrisy of the Jewish leadership, including that of some Pharisees.

Jesus was declared to have uttered blasphemy (Mark 14:64), and the next morning, recast as a political insurrectionist, was transferred to the Roman procurator Pontius Pilate (Mark 15:1). Pilate would hardly have cared about blasphemy, much less conducted a trial concerning it, but a politically threatening prisoner might attract his interest. As for Paul, we must ask if he and Gamaliel attended the night trial. Gamaliel, as a member of the Sanhedrin, could very well have been there. Paul never gives any indication that he was (nor does he ever hint that he had even met or seen the historical Jesus).

The actions of the high priest sent a clear message to Pilate: he and his collaborators wanted Jesus put to death. Since they could not administer capital punishment under Roman rule, the high priest was obviously maneuvering to get Pilate to do his bidding. Everyone who knew the political interplay between the Roman procurator and the high priest would have suspected some deal whereby the high priest got what he wanted but owed a return favor to Pilate, due whenever the procurator was ready to collect. The Jewish leadership was involved in a shady business: a weak sort of power-sharing with the Romans that required cooperation with the very occupiers they resented. Through this crass wheeling and dealing, their status, wealth, and some local power over the temple was maintained, even when their actions helped bring about the death of a poor, yet perhaps very unnerving, itinerant preacher.

Whatever Gamaliel may have seen or heard and discussed with Paul, the case of Jesus may have been hardly worth their attention. A few whose movements came to naught had pretended to be messiahs before. Besides, living in Jerusalem, Gamaliel and Paul were used to how the Romans often solved "problems" with death by crucifixion, especially if the accused was poor. That gruesome punishment was a deterrent, done outside the city walls, far messier and lengthier than the Jewish method of capital punishment—death by stoning.

Were You There When They Crucified My Lord?

Did Paul walk by the hill of Golgotha (Calvary) that fateful day? It is unlikely, since he surely would have said something once he had come to believe that the crucifixion of Jesus was a significant event. Paul has much to say about the death of Jesus in his later letters (for example, 1 Corinthians 2:2) but nothing to indicate he saw the brutal event. It is also doubtful that many other residents of Jerusalem paid much attention to the Romans mockingly parading Jesus through the streets and nailing him on wooden crossbeams. The Romans were always punishing somebody. Golgotha was a regular place for crucifixion.

Was the death of Jesus even talked about among the Pharisees in Paul's circles? It can be suspected not. The Pharisees would have seen Jesus as merely one more Galilean rabble rouser, one more failed candidate to be the awaited messiah. In retrospect, however, Gamaliel may have been hauntingly rattled by Jesus and the treatment meted out to him. The reason to suggest this is that years later, when Peter and others were being interrogated and roughed up by the Sanhedrin, Gamaliel warned the other members: "Have nothing to do with these men, and let them go. For if this endeavor or this activity is of human origin, it will destroy itself. But if it comes from God, you will not be able to destroy them; you may even find yourselves fighting against God" (Acts 5:38–39). Was that advice rooted in a sincere fear of God, perhaps bearing overtones of Gamaliel's unease with the unjust death to which he knew Jesus had been sentenced? Or was it merely a politically expedient warning to not waste energy on the Jesus movement, which he expected to soon die out, as had most other messianic contenders and their followers?

What riveted Paul's attention about the case of Jesus, however, happened not too long after the crucifixion. Initially because of the witness of a woman named Mary of Magdala and some other women, the closest followers of the man from Galilee claimed not only that the tomb of Jesus was empty, as if his body had been stolen, but also that they had encountered him risen from the dead. Led by a man named Peter, the friends who had known Jesus verified the witness of the women based on their encounters with the transformed Jesus.

To Paul, the claim was extremely important since among the Pharisees' most deeply held beliefs, setting them apart from the high priests and Sadducees, was the conviction that God would raise the righteous dead. Now some poor peasant women and fishermen were proclaiming that God had done just that with the crucified Galilean. Although the Pharisees expected the resurrection to take place in one massive event for all the just, Paul could not ignore the passionate and insistent claims about Jesus.

Blasphemy against Moses and God

Early on, the Jesus movement was also called "the Way." As it spread around Jerusalem and was even discussed in the various synagogues of the city, Paul was attentive to it. In the Synagogue of Freedmen, Cyrenians, and Alexandrians that was attended also by people from the provinces of Cilicia and Asia, debates about Jesus were being held, especially with a man named Stephen (Acts 6:9). Paul may have frequented this synagogue, since he was a Cilician and a Greek-speaking Hellenistic Jew, as were its other members. He may have been one of the debaters—and as subsequent events showed—in great disagreement with Stephen's preaching. Acts says that the debaters "could not withstand the wisdom and spirit" with which Stephen spoke (Acts 6:10). Accused of "speaking blasphemous words against Moses and God" (Acts 6:11), Stephen was brought before the Sanhedrin and charged with denying the importance of the temple and the Mosaic law. Further, he was condemned for considering Jesus of more importance than Moses (Acts 6:11–15) and for having predicted the destruction of the temple, as Jesus had (Mark 14:58). Stephen's devaluing of the temple is not surprising given Jesus' critique of those who were its key figures and the failure of the temple in his eyes to be a house of prayer for all people. But this was an unwelcome radical message in Jerusalem. Perhaps that is why even Peter and the other Judean believers in Jesus are not mentioned as coming to Stephen's defense. Perhaps they favored taking a more subtle approach in preaching the implications of the raising of Jesus. Or they might have been afraid.

Paul agreed that Stephen's preaching was blasphemous and that he deserved to be stoned. There is no indication that only a few years after the death of Jesus the Romans were needed to execute a Jewish person condemned for blasphemy. Perhaps the Sanhedrin took matters into their own hands. In any case, Paul was prominently present at the stoning of Stephen outside the city. As Acts depicts the scene, it reports that "the witnesses laid down their cloaks at the feet of a young man named Saul" (Acts 7:58). This implies that Paul did not need to lob rocks at the condemned man; rather, he stood apart near the cloaks, "consenting" (8:1) to Stephen's execution. That Paul's approval was noted tells us that he was considered authoritative, a mature Pharisee.

Setting Out on the Road to Damascus

Turmoil over Stephen's death broke out in Jerusalem that very day. Paul himself was said to have entered house after house, "dragging out men and women" believers to be handed over for imprisonment (Acts 8:3). His view of the Jesus movement may have been formed by how threatening he perceived the preaching about Jesus to be for the Judaism he appreciated so deeply. But also, apart from concurring that Stephen's preaching was blasphemous, Paul would have had numerous intellectual reasons to reject the proclamation that God had raised Jesus from the dead and, as his followers quickly proclaimed, that he was God's awaited Messiah.

As a Pharisee, Paul believed that God would raise all the just who had died, but at a general resurrection at the apocalyptically expected last day. Jesus, proclaimed as raised, was but a single individual. Further, the awaited messiah was expected to lead the Jews to political freedom from the Romans. Jesus had been disappointing on that account; he had not even tried. Moreover, Jesus' death on a cross was considered by the Jews to be a death on a tree. In the view of Deuteronomy 21:23, that form of death was to die the death of a cursed person. Surely, God's messiah would not have had a shameful death.

Once Paul realized that the Jesus movement was spreading far beyond Jerusalem, even into Syria, he went to the high priest and "asked him for letters to the synagogues in Damascus, that, if he should find any men or women who belonged to the Way, he might bring them back to Jerusalem in chains" (Acts 9:1–2). Paul's efforts to protect Judaism were strenuous. As he set out on the long journey to Damascus, was he in an urgent race? Was he in a rage? No doubt he felt he was proceeding with moral justification.

CHAPTER 3

Paul's Revelation: Set Apart and Called

Paul could have traveled the hundred and fifty miles or more from Jerusalem to Damascus via numerous routes. In his hurry, he probably took the least hilly and most well-traveled roads that extended from Jerusalem east to Jericho, then north along the banks of the Jordan River into Galilee. Moving further north along the coast of the Sea of Galilee, he would have turned east to cross the Jordan into the Gamla region of Syria, where he could finally connect to a busy Roman road heading into Damascus. Swaths of well-built Roman roads still survive in wilderness areas of Syria. Somewhere along one of those routes, as Paul drew close to Damascus, an event radically changed his life.

Along the Way

Before closing in on what happened on the road to Damascus, let us think through what may have occurred in the earlier days of the journey. The trip must have taken about a week, even for a zealously energized person "breathing murderous threats" and determined to arrest those he was pursuing (Acts 9:1–2). The journey would have required some logistical planning. Was Paul accompanied? Luke indicates he was (Acts 9:7). Was he walking or on horseback? No one knows, although some artists have added drama to the event by depicting Paul falling from a rearing horse. Were plans made about how far to travel each day and how late it was safe to be on the roads? The barren road from Jerusalem to Jericho wound toward the Dead Sea region through a stretch of uninhabited eroding cliffs. Traveling in such forlorn territory was dangerous, as Jesus portrayed in the parable of the good Samaritan (Luke 10:29–37).

Arriving at the large, vibrant oasis town of Jericho must have been a relief for tired travelers. It would have been easy to find a safe place to bed down and food to purchase. Similarly, accommodations would be easily obtained for the rest of Paul's journey north along the banks of the Jordan and the Sea of Galilee. Once in Syria, however, the parched desert landscape dominated, and although Roman roads converging on the large city of Damascus could be bustling, protected places to stay were few. Paul, ever the extrovert, as his letters in later years reflect, must have camped—and can be imagined conversing late into the night and sharing food and drink around a warm fire with other travelers. Did he tell others about his mission? Did people he encountered sense his fury at the preaching about Christ and the believers in Christ? Had they counterargued with him in Jericho, for example, saying, "But you should see what a changed man Zacchaeus is since Jesus came here" (see Luke 19:1–10), or made comments such as "But wait, he healed so many here; we loved listening to him," or "we can never forget how his teaching touched our hearts." What did Paul hear people say on his route through Jesus' home region of Galilee? Did Paul debate with those attracted to the Galilean peasant and his message? Or rather than argue with this fiery young Pharisee from Jerusalem, did people who encountered him refrain from saying much about Jesus or their own belief? Did Paul perhaps find others along the way who also felt "murderous" toward believers?

Such musings are not unimportant as we try to imagine Paul's state of mind when the revelation took place. It would be enlightening to know if Paul had encountered people who were sympathetic to his anger and to his mission. Perhaps, having sensed belief in Jesus as the Messiah, he became even more upset as he traveled. If Paul encountered heartfelt belief in Jesus Christ, did he become more circumspect, even slightly unsettled about the wisdom of his mission in opposing Christ's followers? Is it possible Paul became more disturbed than ever about the rapidly spreading Jesus movement, or was his certainty jolted? Unfortunately, we have no way of discerning the degree of Paul's certainty in his quest, nor any possible vacillation, as he drew near Damascus. It is recorded that, looking back years later, he was appalled at his zealous actions against believers. In his Letter to the Galatians, he acknowledged that he had "persecuted the church of God beyond measure and tried to destroy it" (1:13). Similarly, in the Letter to the Philippians, he confessed: "in zeal I persecuted the church" (3:6).

Set Apart and Called through Grace

The revelation to Paul on the road to Damascus is one of the most well-known stories of a radical spiritual change of heart, not only in the Bible but in all of world literature as assessed by those who have studied momentous conversions. Paul's words are our primary source for what occurred. In 1 Corinthians, he makes two brief comments. He states in 1 Corinthians 9:1, "Have I not seen Jesus our Lord?" And, in 1 Corinthians 15:8–9, describing how the resurrected Jesus had appeared to Cephas, the twelve, and others, he writes: "Last of all, as to one born abnormally, he appeared to me. For I am the least of the apostles, not fit to be called an apostle, because I persecuted the church of God." In both statements, Paul describes a visual experience.

In his Letter to the Galatians, written before 1 Corinthians, Paul gave a more sustained, although still minimal summary of his experience. Not even mentioning where he was, but implying that he had been heading to Damascus, he summarized the experience in Galatians 1:11–17, a text he wrote almost twenty years after the event.

> Now I want you to know . . . that the gospel preached by me is not of human origin. For I did not receive it from a human being, nor was I taught it, but it came through a revelation of Jesus Christ.
>
> For you heard of my former way of life in Judaism, how I persecuted the church of God beyond measure and tried to destroy it, and progressed

in Judaism beyond many of my contemporaries among my race, since I was even more a zealot for my ancestral traditions. But when [God], who from my mother's womb had set me apart and called me through his grace, was pleased to reveal his Son to me, so that I might proclaim him to the Gentiles, I did not immediately consult flesh and blood, nor did I go up to Jerusalem to those who were apostles before me; rather, I went into Arabia and then returned to Damascus.

Significantly, in verses 12 and 16, Paul describes what happened to him as a revelation (*apokalypsis*, Greek, meaning to remove the veil). God had caused him to encounter the resurrected Christ. This profound experience with the Risen One shattered Paul's denial that God had raised Jesus from the dead. As a faithful Jew, Paul had staunchly believed that the resurrection of the dead would not take place until the end of time. What could he now say to argue that God had not raised Jesus? Nothing, for through God's revelation, he had encountered the resurrected Lord.

Paul's profound experience of the risen Christ prompted a rethinking of his understanding of Judaism. Rethinking does not, however, mean rejecting. And rethinking also takes time. In his letters, we see Paul working out the implications of his belief in the resurrection of Jesus for the rest of his life. Paul never says that he abandoned his Jewish faith nor his Pharisaic identity. Notably, by saying that he had been set apart since his birth, he indicated that his call echoed that of the prophet Jeremiah, who wrote: "The word of the LORD came to me: / Before I formed you in the womb I knew you, / before you were born I dedicated you, / a prophet to the nations I appointed you" (Jeremiah 1:4–5).

Now, in the event on the road to Damascus, God gave Paul a new lens through which he would express his faith and worship: God had indeed raised Jesus. For Paul, the theological implications were profound, implications that he long pondered and gradually articulated in the letters he wrote to early Christian communities.

Paul's experience on the road to Damascus has often been referred to as his conversion. That is not an adequate term to use, however, since it suggests changing from one faith to another. It can also imply a rejection of what one formerly believed. Paul's revelation, on the contrary, was quite different, although his life was indeed turned radically. He had been a deeply moral, committed person in the Pharisaic, Jewish context; he remained the same moral Pharisaic Jewish man as a Christ believer. But now he had transitioned into that sect of Jewish believers, called Nazarenes, or followers of the Way. They were that group, one of numerous Jewish sects at the time, who recognized that Jesus had been raised by God and whom they now called Messiah and Lord.

Now, in the event on the road to Damascus, God gave Paul a new lens through which he would express his faith and worship: God had indeed raised Jesus.

After believers came to be called Christians, Paul would be called a Jewish Christian, and because he was Greek-speaking and from the diaspora, he would be identified as a Hellenistic Jewish Christian. Regarding a shift in his morality, we can observe that yes, the people he had intended to round up in Damascus and return to Jerusalem would have received the legal Jewish capital punishment for blasphemy—stoning—as did Stephen (Acts 7:54–60). That would not have been considered murder, however; as strange as it may seem today, it was moral in the context of Jewish law. But after Paul's revelation, he no longer judged believers in the resurrected Christ to be blasphemous; he had become one of them. Then, according to Luke's recording in the Acts of the Apostles, Paul described his old self as having been "murderous" toward innocent believers (Acts 9:1). In hindsight, Paul must have felt he had made a terrible mistake, although blameless at the time, in his pursuit of innocent believers.

A Thrice-Told Tale

Acts offers more extensive information about the revelation to Paul on the road to Damascus. Luke tells the story three times, with slight variations, and embeds the event in different ways within his narrative: in Acts 9:1–9; 22:3–16; and 26:2–18. How had Luke learned so many details that are not found in Paul's letters? Possibly from Paul himself, but more likely he had heard slightly different versions of Paul's call experience from the oral tradition among the Christians. Since Luke was writing Acts late in the first century, it should be kept in mind that what Paul experienced on the road to Damascus in the mid-30s had, by the time of Luke's writing, undergone decades of retelling, perhaps with some additional interpretive slants. These interpretive slants become evident when comparing the three excerpts below.

In Acts 9:4–9, Luke tells the story of Paul's revelation, stating that the event occurred near Damascus when a light from the sky flashed around Paul:

> He fell to the ground and heard a voice saying to him, "Saul, Saul, why are you persecuting me?" He said, "Who are you, sir?" The reply came, "I am Jesus, whom you are persecuting. Now get up and go into the city and you will be told what you must do." The men who were traveling with him stood speechless, for they heard the voice but could see no one. Saul got up from the ground, but when he opened his eyes he could see nothing; so they led him by the hand and brought him to Damascus. For three days he was unable to see, and he neither ate nor drank.

This straightforward account portrays both Paul and the men with him hearing the voice.

The second, far-more-detailed account (Acts 22:6–16), embeds the story in Paul's defense before Jews after his arrest in Jerusalem. Here, Luke portrays Paul as telling the story:

> On that journey as I drew near to Damascus, about noon a great light from the sky suddenly shone around me. I fell to the ground and heard a voice saying to me, "Saul, Saul, why are you persecuting me?" I replied, "Who are you, sir?" And he said to me, "I am Jesus the Nazorean whom you are persecuting." My companions saw the light but did not hear the voice of the one who spoke to me. I asked, "What shall I do, sir?" The Lord answered me, "Get up and go into Damascus, and there you will be told about everything appointed for you to do." Since I could

> see nothing because of the brightness of that light, I was led by hand by my companions and entered Damascus.

Paul's companions saw the light around Paul but heard nothing. It is probably not significant that in the prior version the men heard but could not see while in this second accounting they could see but not hear; small variations in a story most likely reflect differences in the oral tradition. In this second narrative, Paul asks Jesus what he should do, and Jesus says he will be told about "everything appointed for you to do." "Appointment" suggests a divine role given to someone by God, a more momentous way of expressing it than in the first version's phrasing, "you will be told what you must do" (Acts 9:6). This variation likely comes from Luke's editing.

Finally, in Acts 26:12–19 Luke narrates the story again, as told by Paul in his defense to King Agrippa and his consort Queen Berenice[1] during his trial in Caesarea:

> I was traveling to Damascus with the authorization and commission of the chief priests. At midday, along the way, O king, I saw a light from the sky, brighter than the sun, shining around me and my traveling companions. We all fell to the ground and I heard a voice saying to me in Hebrew, "Saul, Saul, why are you persecuting me? It is hard for you to kick against the goad." And I said, "Who are you, sir?" And the Lord replied, "I am Jesus whom you are persecuting. Get up now, and stand on your feet. I have appeared to you for this purpose, to appoint you as a servant and witness of what you have seen [of me] and what you will be shown. I shall deliver you from this people and from the Gentiles to whom I send you, to open their eyes that they may turn from darkness to light and from the power of Satan to God, so that they may obtain forgiveness of sins and an inheritance among those who have been consecrated by faith in me."
>
> And so, King Agrippa, I was not disobedient to the heavenly vision.[2]

---

1. See Florence Morgan Gillman, "Berenice as Paul's Witness to the Resurrection (Acts 25–26)," in *Resurrection in the New Testament: Festschrift J. Lambrecht*, ed. R. Bieringer, (Bibliotheca Ephemeridum Theologicarum Lovaniensium, 2002), 249–264.
2. This magnificent speech and the discussion in its aftermath continues in Acts 26:20–32.

With far more visual details and imagery than the two previous narratives, this version highlights Luke's verbal prowess in formal speech writing. A political note is evident, perhaps of interest to a king, that Paul's mission was authorized and commissioned. In this version, Paul does not have to wait until he is in Damascus to discover why Jesus had appeared to him. Deliverance from "this people"—namely, Jewish opposition—and from Gentiles is also promised in the future for Paul for the salvation of all, that future having already taken place as Paul spoke. In the telling of the event on the road to Damascus, Paul has placed words of Jesus that portray much of what would later come to pass.

These three narratives show that Luke tailored the account to the context, keeping some details consistent and varying others. While the core of the appearance story remains intact in all three accounts, it is not surprising to find these editorial characteristics in the work of an ancient historian such as Luke. Modest adaptation was quite acceptable. Our modern demand for more consistently precise data may not be met by Luke's texts. To be fair to the evangelist, however, his scholarly intention in the two-volume narrative (his Gospel account and Acts) was based upon his having investigated "everything accurately anew" and his purpose was "to write it down in an orderly sequence" (Luke 1:3).

"Now get up and go into the city . . ." (Acts 9:6)

Luke, rather than Paul, tells about the immediate aftermath of Paul's revelation (Acts 9:10–19; 22:12–16). Once in Damascus, Paul was taken to the house of a man named Judas who lived on a street called Straight. A devout Jewish man and a Christ follower named Ananias arrived, laid hands on Paul, and cured his blindness. Paul was then baptized. Luke adds the very human observation that "when he had eaten, he recovered his strength" (Acts 9:19).

We might imagine ourselves in Paul's place. Was his intellect shocked that God had indeed raised Jesus? Was he spiritually humbled because the Lord had forcefully touched his life? Was he feeling regretful about the self-righteous mission to arrest believers that he had originally set out upon? What did it mean that Paul would be sent to the Gentiles (Acts 26:17)? Was he not a Pharisee trained to teach the Jews? Was Paul wondering what he was to do next? Luke says that he stayed a few days with the Christ believers in Damascus and then "he began at once to proclaim Jesus in the synagogues, that he is the Son of God" (Acts 9:20).

"For you will be his witness before all to what you have seen and heard" (Acts 22:15)

How was it possible that just a few days after the event on the road to Damascus Paul reversed his stance and began to preach that Jesus was indeed God's Son? To understand this sharp turn from a man who persecuted Christ believers to one who preached Christ crucified and risen, let us consider the lens through which Paul viewed the world. As previously discussed, Paul was a Pharisee who had studied Scripture, tradition, and the law at the highest level. All of that remained in place for him intellectually; but now, through experiencing an encounter with God, Paul had acquired a new lens through which to view what he knew and believed: the resurrected Christ. From then on, he would use the revelation given to him as a filter for his understanding of the covenant with God, the writings of the prophets, and the expectations of the Messiah. He would do this in his preaching and teaching for the rest of his life. Yes, he was ready to preach about Jesus soon after the event on the road to Damascus. God had indeed confirmed Paul's knowledge of Judaism and his Pharisaic expectation that God would raise the dead. Fortunately, Paul' subsequent letters help us grasp how he theologically came to understand and formulate for others the identity and significance of the death and resurrection of Jesus. His was a mission for which he was well equipped.

For more than two millennia, Paul's experience on the road to Damascus has maintained its seminal importance in writings on Christian theology and spirituality. Preachers and scholars have interpreted the event and its implications for believers throughout history. Many Christians have also accompanied Paul on this road in a spiritual sense; some have wished for a similar encounter with Jesus—they have desired the same clarity of faith in the risen Lord. Artists also have been fascinated by Paul's experience. They have often assumed that he, as a likely well-off person, was on horseback and have depicted his horse rearing in fright at the searing light that blinded him. The startled horse becomes the artist's explanation of what made Paul fall to the ground. Some artists have shown him surrounded by a few or many companions. But what remains inexpressible on canvas (as we will see when we discuss Paul's subsequent life) is the extraordinary spiritual and psychological thrust, the relentless, energetic drive to witness to the resurrected Lord that Paul's profound revelation sustained in him throughout the next three difficult and dangerous decades of his life.

Recall that Paul concluded his words about his stay in Damascus by noting: "I did not immediately consult flesh and blood [that is, people who had known Jesus], nor did I go up to Jerusalem to those who were apostles before me; rather, I went into Arabia and then returned to Damascus" (Galatians 1:16–17). Here, Arabia refers to the region of the Nabatean Arabs, a land to the east and south of Damascus, ruled then by King Aretas IV. Paul may have preached in that region for a few years and—characteristically as we shall often see—stirred up controversy that came to the attention of the king. This is reflected in Paul's description of his escape: "At Damascus the governor under King Aretas guarded the city of Damascus in order to seize me, but I was lowered in a basket through a window in a wall and escaped his hands" (2 Corinthians 11:32–33).

Return to Tarsus

With the escape from Damascus, Paul was then on his way back to Jerusalem for the first time since leaving a few years earlier, furiously intent on rounding up believers. Now he was returning as one of them. When Paul reached Jerusalem, however, "he tried to join the disciples, but they were all afraid of him, not believing that he was a disciple" (Acts 9:26). It was Barnabas who vouched for Paul's sincerity and whose words led to Paul's initial acceptance among the believers. Based on Barnabas' assurance, Paul was able to interact with the apostles and preach in Jerusalem. All did not go smoothly, however. He "debated with the Hellenists, but they tried to kill him" (Acts 9:29). This may indicate that Paul had returned to the Greek-speaking synagogue where Stephen had preached and had been rejected for blasphemy. In any case, Paul's early preaching in the city caused an uproar, so when the disciples learned of this "they took him down to [the seaport of] Caesarea and sent him on his way to Tarsus" (Acts 9:30).

Based on Barnabas' assurance, Paul was able to interact with the apostles and preach in Jerusalem.

Around the year 40, Paul would have left Jerusalem to return home to Tarsus, probably for the first time since he had traveled to Jerusalem decades earlier to study. What an amazing life trajectory he had lived so far! He had studied with a great teacher, become one himself, encountered the resurrected Lord, and preached in the great cities of Damascus and Jerusalem. Now he was returning to his roots, perhaps to occasional preaching in and around Tarsus, and to tent-making, perhaps in the family business. Considering that Paul was now a mature, even older man given the life expectancy of his times, we might wonder if he felt that he was being put out to pasture, exiled by the Jerusalem disciples into retirement. His interpretation of events is unknowable, and there is no evidence of his activities for about the next five years. Were these quiet, uneventful years a slow slide into retirement and old age? If so, it is possible he was surprised by the next developments in his ministry.

Chapter 4

Paul's Mission and Teachings

When Paul arrived in Tarsus after being sent there by the disciples in Jerusalem, he likely returned to work in the tent-making business. He may also have reconnected with the Jewish community of his childhood. Were the local Jews open to his preaching or did they treat him like a prophet unappreciated in his own town? (See for example, Matthew 13:54–58 in the comments Jesus made about his rejection in Nazareth.) Paul surely evangelized in the regions surrounding Tarsus as well. Yet nothing is known for certain about his life from roughly the years 40 to 45.

In Acts 11:19–26, Luke recounts what happened around the end of those five years: A controversy had developed in Syria in the city of Antioch between Jewish followers of Jesus and a sizable number of Greeks who were believers. Whether by the word *Greeks* Luke means Hellenistic Jewish believers or Greek-speaking Gentiles who had come to faith in Jesus is unclear; either way their controversy came to the attention of the Jerusalem church. The Jerusalem elders sent Barnabas, himself a Hellenistic Jewish believer originally from Cyprus, to investigate. His mediation was successful, since "a large number of people was added to the Lord" (Acts 11:24), but Barnabas knew he needed another bilingual, multicultural person to help him minister within the church of Antioch. Thinking to enlist Paul, Barnabas traveled eighty-five miles or so west. He may have thought Paul would need some persuasion after his difficult time in Jerusalem. Paul, however, accepted the summons to go to the church of Antioch, and for a year, he and Barnabas taught there together. Luke ends his account of this period in Antioch by noting that it was there that "the disciples were first called Christians" (Acts 11:26). While Paul never uses this name for himself or for any believers, he must have known the term.

The Years with Barnabas

From this period in Antioch forward, and for some four years (between about 45 and 49), Barnabas and Paul worked together. Initially, they were sent by the church in Antioch to Jerusalem to deliver aid for famine-stricken Judeans. In Jerusalem a younger man named John, also called Mark, became their companion. (Some scholars think he is the same Mark who, around 70, wrote the Gospel according to Mark). Upon their arrival back in Antioch, the church there sensed the Spirit was telling them: "Set apart for me Barnabas and Saul for the work to which I have called them" (Acts 13:2). So the church in Antioch sent the three off from the nearby port of Seleucia. Their initial destination was the port of Salamis in Cyprus, Barnabas' home region. Thus began the first of what we now refer to as Paul's three missionary journeys.

The events of Paul's life referred to in this book so far have taken place along the eastern regions of the Mediterranean Sea, the area known as the Levant. We have followed Paul's movements to and from Tarsus, Jerusalem, Damascus, the Arabian desert, Antioch, and finally back to Tarsus. Setting off with Barnabas, Paul was about to launch a missionary career taking him much farther afield, covering vast swaths of the Roman Empire.

Recounting these journeys with all their amazing details is beyond the scope of this brief text. Biblical scholarship has taken up this endeavor and compiled the fascinating stories about Paul's evangelizing, based upon both his many epistles and the long narrative about his travels by Luke in Acts 13:4—28:30. Many books have been written for those who would like an almost blow-by-blow recounting of Paul's journeys, which encompass the latter two decades or so of his life (that is, the years from the mid-40s to the mid-60s).[1] Maps in many study Bibles and also online detail Paul's travels. Consulting some of these will provide a visual dimension for the following chapters where I will touch on some highlights of Paul's travels and note some major controversies that arose.

The standard division of Paul's work into three missionary journeys, followed by a final voyage when he was taken as a prisoner to Rome, is mainly a construct modern readers impose upon the text to follow his missionary work. Scholars have long observed that Luke's narrative about Paul's travels, starting from when he and Barnabas headed to Cyprus, seems to fall into three parts (Acts 13:4—14:28; 15:40—18:22; and 18:23—26:32), thus the concept of three journeys. That division makes sense, since at the close of each section, Paul ends up back in either Antioch or Jerusalem. But we cannot be certain Paul saw his almost nonstop missionary activity in such a compartmentalized way. He was a man whose passion to witness to the risen Christ amazes; he was so driven by his call to preach about Jesus that he rarely stayed long in any one place (2 Corinthians 5:14: "For the love of Christ impels us"). As noted in the previous chapter, there was an extraordinary thrust, a relentless, energetic drive within him ever since his experience on the road to Damascus.

However, another fascinating factor was at play. Just as when Paul first preached in Jerusalem, during his missionary journeys he regularly met opposition from both Jews and Gentiles, even to the point of facing physical danger. His preaching elicited such strong reactions from listeners—not only positive but also negative—that he was often escorted or driven out of places where he had evangelized. Other conflicts emerged as well. When Paul first traveled with Barnabas, John Mark accompanied them. Yet, for reasons unknown, John Mark departed from them along the way. That departure seems to have been caused by a falling out, and when Barnabas wanted

1. See, for example, Scholz, Daniel J., *The Pauline Letters: Introducing the New Testament* (Winona, MN: Anselm Academic, 2013).

John Mark to accompany them on a second journey, Paul refused to continue with them (Acts 15:37–38). Also, while Paul and Barnabas seem to have remained congenial, they went their separate ways as evangelizers. The break with Barnabas became the occasion for Paul to enlist other traveling companions such as Silvanus, Sosthenes, and Timothy, whose names we find especially in the greetings and closing salutations of his letters (see for example, 1 Corinthians 1:1; 2 Corinthians 1:1; Philippians 1:1; 1 Thessalonians 1:1; Philemon 1:1).

Paul's Method of Evangelizing

On Paul's many travels, he generally tried to connect first with the Jewish residents of a place. Especially in his early itinerant years, Paul felt an allegiance to his people and believed that his message should first be directed to them. After all, he was proclaiming the resurrection of a Jewish man, a descendant of David, as the Jewish Messiah, the Son of the God of the Jews. If a town or city had a synagogue or some other Jewish meeting place, such as a gathering spot for prayer, Paul sought out that venue.

Yet among his own people, Paul often encountered strong negative reactions, controversy, and disbelief. While Paul's interactions often became so dangerous that he and his companions were driven or secretly taken out of town, at other times Paul became so infuriated at the Jewish resistance that he preached instead in a public place to anyone who would listen (see Acts 13: 44–52). Sometimes that also resulted in threats or even violence. Yet, for those who gave Paul a hearing and believed, vibrant groups of Christ believers were formed, groups comprising both Jews and Gentiles. The seismic development of his outright preaching to the Gentiles can hardly be stressed enough: "It was necessary that the word of God be spoken to you first, but since you reject it and condemn yourselves as unworthy of eternal life, we now turn to the Gentiles" (Acts 13:46).

Already during Paul's travels with Barnabas, the two missionaries encountered numerous Gentiles who welcomed their message.

They were not the first evangelizers of Christ to accept Gentiles as members of their small groups of believers; Peter was known to have converted Cornelius, a Roman centurion, and his family (Acts 10). Possibly some of the "Greeks" who had already converted in the Antiochian church were Gentiles too. In these early years of the expansion of Christianity, Gentile believers certainly seem to have been welcomed but they were also seen as exceptions to the norm, the Jewish Christians. Believers in Jesus were, by far, predominantly Jewish. Yet, experiencing that the Spirit of God had brought a few Gentiles to belief was convincing to evangelizers such as Peter, Paul, and Barnabas that these exceptions were to be welcomed and absorbed in the wider movement.

Judaism in the diaspora already had a long tradition of proselytizing, seeking some Gentile converts. Those who wished to convert were known as God-fearers; they shared Jewish belief, prayed with the Jews, and gradually adopted Jewish practices associated with dietary and marriage laws. Some Gentile God-fearers, however, never became fully Jewish, especially some men, since they were undoubtedly aware that the requirement to be circumcised could endanger their lives. Nonetheless, the Jewish community still welcomed God-fearers who did not complete the conversion process, although they no doubt felt second class.

Upon their return to Antioch, Paul and Barnabas reported their success in making conversions: "They called the church together and reported what God had done with them and how he had opened the door of faith to the Gentiles" (Acts 14:27). Dissension arose, however, between the two missionaries and visiting Jewish Christians from Judea who had been instructing the Antiochians: "Unless you are circumcised according to the Mosaic practice, you cannot be saved" (Acts 15:1). Yet Paul and Barnabas had made a judgment that circumcision was not necessary for their numerous male Gentile converts. Looking back at this significant turning point in early Christianity, the seismic nature of their decision is apparent. They, however, may not have realized the extraordinary impact Gentile believers would have upon the Jesus movement.

"After much debate . . ." (Acts 15:7)

Such a momentous development among the believers needed to be validated in consultation with the apostolic leadership. Thus, the Antiochian church decided that Paul, Barnabas, and others should "go up to Jerusalem to the apostles and presbyters about this question" (Acts 15:2). This occasioned what, in retrospect, is called the Council of Jerusalem. The year was about 50. Some see this as the first of the many church councils throughout the history of Christianity, the most recent of which was the Second Vatican Council (1962–65, convened by Pope John XXIII). The Council of Jerusalem reflects that, from the beginning, believers sensed the necessity for mutual consultation to safeguard the unity of their fledgling movement.

The Council of Jerusalem reflects that, from the beginning, believers sensed the necessity for mutual consultation to safeguard the unity of their fledgling movement.

Luke tells the story of this council in Acts 15. First, he reports that some Pharisees who had become believers held the traditional position: "It is necessary to circumcise them [the Gentiles] and direct them to observe the Mosaic law" (Acts 15:5). This set the stage for a series of speeches by Peter, Paul, Barnabas, and James the brother of the Lord, leader of the Jerusalem group. None of these latter speakers, for varying reasons, thought that circumcision should be required of Gentile converts. James, however, favored imposing some Jewish dietary and marriage laws upon the converts, although there is little evidence that these were widely enforced. Thus, the die had been cast, the work of the Spirit had been validated: the door welcoming the Gentiles had been declared open. It is unlikely, though, that they realized they had opened the floodgates.

The Apocalyptic Paul and the Gentiles

Since Paul thoroughly understood Judaism, he was attuned to the apocalyptic sense, which for some centuries had intensified the hopes for a messiah. Pharisees such as Paul, who studied the Hebrew prophets, encountered a variety of ideas about what the messiah, or even more than one messiah as some thought, would be like. In general, the expectation was that the messiah would usher in the final days, during which God's reign would be fully established. This was also referred to as "the day of the Lord." At that time, all the just would be resurrected and evil defeated once and for all. John the Baptist had preached apocalyptically, stating that the inbreaking of the reign of God was at hand. Jesus, whose preaching followed John's, taught in the same vein: "After John had been arrested, Jesus came to Galilee proclaiming the gospel of God: This is the time of fulfillment. The kingdom of God is at hand. Repent, and believe in the gospel" (Mark 1:15).

Paul understood that with the end so near, one should concentrate on preparation for the return of the Lord. Paul expected to still be alive when the Lord returned.

The theological implications of joining in the believers' recognition of Jesus as the Messiah were momentous for Paul. True, only Jesus had been raised from the dead, which meant there was so much yet to unfold in the end-time events ushered in by his resurrection. As Paul would later write, he came to the conviction that Jesus was "the firstborn of the dead" (Colossians 1:18), "the firstborn among many brothers" (Romans 8:29), and that the anticipated resurrection of all the just was imminent. Paul's preaching was thus decidedly apocalyptic. Many of his recommendations were made in the light of the end coming at any moment. One well-known example is his recommendation of celibacy to the Corinthians if they could live that way (1 Corinthians 7:8). Paul understood that with the end so near, one should concentrate on preparation for the return of the Lord. Paul expected to still be alive when the Lord returned (1 Thessalonians 4:15).

Another aspect of Paul's apocalypticism came from his knowledge of the writing of the prophet Isaiah. Of all the prophets Paul quotes, Isaiah is cited most frequently.[2] With Isaiah, Paul would have shared in the expectation that in the messiah's time the nations would be converted:

> In days to come,
> The mountain of the LORD's house
> shall be established as the highest mountain
> and raised above the hills.
> All nations shall stream toward it.
> Many peoples shall come and say:
> "Come, let us go up to the LORD's mountain,
> to the house of the God of Jacob,
> That he may instruct us in his ways,
> and we may walk in his paths."
> For from Zion shall go forth instruction,
> and the word of the LORD from Jerusalem. (Isaiah 2:2–3)

For a Jew to speak of "nations" was to speak of all Gentiles. From Isaiah, Paul was convinced that now that the messiah had come in the person of Jesus, the Gentiles too were intended to become his followers. Isaiah's prophetic message confirmed for Paul that his preaching to the nations was divinely mandated, just as reports of the revelation on the road to Damascus had established.

"We shall always be with the Lord"

Paul looked forward with great expectation to Jesus' second coming, for which he used the Greek term *parousia*, meaning "coming." In 1 Thessalonians 4:13—5:11, Paul writes one of his most descriptive passages about the day of the Lord, with a portion of that text allaying the concerns of the Thessalonians who feared for their loved ones

2. On the importance of Isaiah to Paul, the New Testament, and early Christianity, see especially Richard J. Clifford, *Thus Says the Lord: The Prophets in the Liturgy* (Chicago: Liturgy Training Publications, 2021), 82–96.

who had already died. This comforting text lays to rest the thought that those who died before Christ's return would be at a disadvantage:

> We do not want you to be unaware, brothers, about those who have fallen asleep, so that you may not grieve like the rest, who have no hope. For if we believe that Jesus died and rose, so too will God, through Jesus, bring with him those who have fallen asleep. Indeed, we tell you this, on the word of the Lord, that we who are alive, who are left until the coming of the Lord, will surely not precede those who have fallen asleep. For the Lord himself, with a word of command, with the voice of an archangel and with the trumpet of God, will come down from heaven, and the dead in Christ will rise first. Then we who are alive, who are left, will be caught up together with them in the clouds to meet the Lord in the air. Thus we shall always be with the Lord. Therefore console one another with these words. (1 Thessalonians 4:13–18)

Paul taught that Christians' grief should be different from those who have no hope. As he understood it, what matters about the future is that "we shall always be with the Lord" (1 Thessalonians 4:17).

Paul, Slavery, and the End

Paul's apparent acceptance of slavery is another example of the influence of apocalypticism on his thinking and teaching. He has often been criticized for not speaking clearly against this social institution. Paul was not a social reformer for the long term; he did not expect there to be a long term. His teaching concerned preparation for the imminent return of Jesus.

Enforced by the Romans, slavery was thoroughly embedded in the cultures Paul moved among. It was a key part of the social fabric. This does not mean Paul approved of it wholeheartedly, and he certainly thought one should gain freedom if possible. In 1 Corinthians 7:21–24, Paul writes:

> Were you a slave when you were called? Do not be concerned but, even if you can gain your freedom, make the most of it. For the slave called in the Lord is a freed person in the Lord, just as the free person who has been

called is a slave of Christ. You have been purchased at a price. Do not become slaves to human beings. Brothers, everyone should continue before God in the state in which he was called.

In the last sentence, we especially feel the impact of apocalypticism. Since Paul considered the time before the end to be short, he advised remaining in one's present state in life; what mattered was an individual's inner freedom to be committed to Christ. This same thought is evident in the various instances in which Paul describes himself as a "slave [Greek *doulos*] of Christ" (for example, Romans 1:1; Philippians 1:1). In these statements he inwardly identified with slavery positively since his master was the Lord. (Because of the painful history of slavery in the United States, however, some recommend translating the Greek term *doulos* as servant rather than slave.)

Paul most directly addresses slavery in his Letter to Philemon.[3] In this brief document (only twenty-five verses), the imprisoned Paul writes to a house church host and slave owner, Philemon, concerning the owner's runaway slave Onesimus. It appears that Onesimus, after escaping from Philemon and perhaps stealing from him, found his way, whether accidentally or intentionally, to the imprisoned Paul. Under Paul's influence, Philemon became a Christian and a great help to Paul in his confinement, so much so that Paul may have wanted Philemon to let Onesimus remain permanently with him. Yet Paul, perhaps with Roman laws about harboring runaway slaves in mind, and possibly hoping Philemon would willingly give Onesimus to him, sent the young man back to Philemon.

Paul offered to pay restitution for whatever Onesimus had stolen. Above all, Paul wanted Philemon to treat Onesimus no longer as a slave but as a brother in Christ. There is some interesting social pressure applied in the conclusion to this letter when Paul says that he trusted in Philemon's compliance but added: "At the same time prepare a guest room for me, for I hope to be granted to you through

3. See Florence Morgan Gillman, "Philemon," in José Enrique Aguilar Chiu, et al., eds., *The Paulist Biblical Commentary* (Mahwah, NJ, 2018), 1480–1482.

your prayers" (Philemon 22). So Paul planned to check up on which course of action Philemon took!

What Will the Neighbors Think?

In the case of Onesimus, it can be seen that Paul, though primarily not a social reformer, realized that what he asked of Philemon would likely be difficult and cause him local problems. If Philemon started treating his slave as a brother in Christ, and if, as Paul may have been hoping, he freed him to return to Paul, what would Philemon's other slaves or neighboring slave owners' slaves have thought? Was conversion not a way to better treatment and to freedom? And how would other slave owners react to Philemon? Was Paul not upsetting the social balance between owners and slaves? But if Philemon did not treat Onesimus as a brother and send him to Paul, how would Paul react? After all, Paul reminds Philemon, "You owe me your very self" (Philemon 19), meaning he must have attributed his conversion to Paul.

The dilemma reflected in this brief letter is a classic one for Christians, in which one is going to be criticized whether one acts as a Christian should or fails to act.

CHAPTER 5

Paul's Coworkers and Opponents

With their mission to the Gentiles approved by the Council of Jerusalem, both Paul and Barnabas were ready to set forth again upon their return to Antioch, traveling most likely late in the year 50. They set out to evangelize on separate routes, however, because of their disagreement about John Mark accompanying them. Another point of tension between them may also have become a factor since Barnabas, like Peter, was known to have had some reservations about eating with Gentiles. Paul had once challenged this publicly (Galatians 2:12). Going his separate way, Barnabas took John Mark with him; and little is known about Barnabas' subsequent evangelizing. Some years later, however, Paul mentions him (1 Corinthians 9:6), reflecting Paul's ongoing esteem for his earlier mentor.

When Paul left Antioch, he was accompanied by Silas (also called Silvanus). In the following eight years or so, Paul would travel extensively through the Roman provinces encompassing present-day Turkey and Greece, returning only once to Antioch and twice to Jerusalem (on maps this travel comprises his second and third journeys). Besides Silas, he was accompanied at different times by other trusted believers, such as Timothy and Titus. Occasionally Paul left behind one of these companions, whom he called his *synergoi* (Greek, coworkers). They were to shepherd the new groups of believers for a time and then catch up with Paul; in each place where he began a church, he also developed local leadership. The hosts of his house churches, both male and female, were presumably the main leaders. Paul was dependent on his coworkers and local leaders, and his letters and Acts reflect that he was generally collaborative and appreciative of them; toward opponents, however, he could exhibit a fiery anger.

Bringing Paul's Coworkers Out of the Shadows

Unfortunately, many of Paul's collaborators have not been well known among Christians. That is often because the texts in which they are mentioned have not been included in the lectionary readings for Sunday Masses, with their proclamation only at weekday Masses or omitted altogether. Texts about women, especially, have been rarely highlighted in homilies or catechesis. Paul's female collaborators, as well as his female friends and acquaintances[1] who have remained in the shadows include, for example, the deacon Phoebe; the household heads Lydia and Nympha; the mother and daughter pair, Lois and Eunice; the church leaders Euodia and Syntychē; and Junia, wife of Andronicus, a couple whom Paul described as "prominent among the apostles" (Romans 16:7).

Regrettably, having never heard of these people, many have assumed that women and married couples did not have leadership roles in ministry in the early churches. Quite the opposite is true. Let us turn to some descriptions of a few of Paul's coworkers.

Based on evidence from the epistles and Acts, it is critical to emphasize that in his relationships with coworkers, Paul was a collaborator, and certainly in no way autocratic in his interactions with those around him. This is reflected in his attitudes toward both men and women. Also, Paul never states that leaders of his churches or leaders of their local Eucharistic celebrations, for example, had to be male. When he uses the rare terms *overseers* and *ministers* (*episkopoi* and *diakonoi*, Greek, overseers and ministers; the latter should be literally translated as "deacon" although some use "minister," as in Philippians 1:1), Paul does not differentiate by gender. Both masculine plural terms serve to include females as well. It is, therefore, unfair to Paul that some later readers of the epistles cast him as a male

1. See Florence M. Gillman, *Women Who Knew Paul* (Collegeville, MN: Liturgical Press, 1992).

chauvinist and a misogynist. There will be more to comment about this charge in the context of discussing the authorship of his letters.

Phoebe of Cenchreae

A fascinating case in point of a coworker is Phoebe, whom Paul describes in Romans 16:1–2. At the time of his writing Romans, Paul was in Corinth making plans to travel to Rome for his first visit. The Letter to the Romans was his introduction to the Roman Christians since he had not founded that church. Phoebe, who lived in Corinth's eastern seaport, Cenchreae, was planning a trip there and was to deliver Paul's missive. Paul voices his confidence in Phoebe, stating:

> I commend to you Phoebe our sister [*adelphē*], who is a minister [*diakonos*] of the church at Cenchreae, that you may receive her in the Lord in a manner worthy of the holy ones and help her in whatever she may need from you, for she has been a benefactor [*prostatis*] to many and to me as well.

From this text we can glean much information. Phoebe's name is an epithet for the goddess Artemis, thus suggesting she was a Gentile convert, a sister, *adelphē,* in Christ. For her to have been a benefactor, *prostatis,* she must have been rather well off, perhaps with a home large enough to host church gatherings and resources to also help Paul. In light of this, her trip to Rome suggests she may have been a businesswoman. Her status as a *diakonos* is significant. Note that this term is translated as minister here; it may also be translated literally as deacon but not deaconess. That latter female form is not found in Greek until four centuries later, and by then, the term had a more specific connotation designating a ministry by and for women. Further, it would be unfair to Paul's Greek and his esteem for this person to call her a deaconess since, owing to later Christian history, deaconesses had a role lesser than that of a male deacon, a distinction Paul did not make. Paul describes himself and many others with the term *diakonos* (see, for example, 1 Corinthians 3:5; 2 Corinthians 3:6; 6:4; 11:23; 1 Thessalonians 3:2) in the same egalitarian sense with which he refers to Phoebe. In contemporary Roman Catholic discussions advocating the revival of the ordination of female deacons, Phoebe is, of course, well known.

Prisca and Aquila of Rome, Corinth, and Ephesus

Among Paul's other esteemed coworkers were the couple Prisca (diminutive Priscilla) and Aquila. Much data can be pieced together about them. Paul came to know them, like Phoebe, during his stay in Corinth. They had moved there from Rome because around 49, the emperor Claudius had driven many Jews out of the city, owing to disturbances in synagogues, apparently because of disruptive preaching about Christ. Aquila was a Jew originally from Pontus (now northern Turkey) and Prisca, based on her Roman name, was likely a Gentile. Based on studies of Roman names, hers suggests she was from a social class higher than Aquila's Jewish status. Possibly, she had also received some education and may have been a scribe for Paul.[2] Prisca and Aquila were already believers in the Lord when they moved to Corinth. As tentmakers, they easily found work there and Paul connected with them through those artisan channels, living and working along with them.

As a city on one end of a narrow isthmus with two seaports, Lechaion on the west and Cenchreae on the east, and a transit road (the famous *diolkos,* paved trackway) connecting the two, Corinth was an epicenter of action. Paul was in Corinth initially for a rather long period, some eighteen months between 50 and 51. He followed his time there with a lengthy correspondence of which we have at least the two letters now named 1 and 2 Corinthians. Much can be pieced together about the Corinthian church and even various named members. This church was vibrant, feisty, challenging, and

2. See Florence M. Gillman, "1 Thessalonians," in Florence M. Gillman, Mary Ann Beavis and HyeRan Kim-Cragg, *1—2 Thessalonians* (*Wisdom Commentary* 52; Collegeville: Liturgical Press, 2016), 28–29

gave Paul much grief and, only occasionally, consolation. Prisca and Aquila were there from 50 through 51, apparently hosting a house church, likely one of several in the city and region. They would certainly have known Phoebe.

Paul decided to leave Corinth sometime in 51 and work his long way back to Antioch in Syria via Ephesus and Caesarea (Acts 18:18–23; this would mark the ending of Paul's second journey). Prisca and Aquila traveled with him as far as Ephesus. Paul kept going and, after disembarking in Caesarea and stopping in Jerusalem, returned overland to Antioch. Meanwhile in Ephesus, the couple became involved in a synagogue and probably established a house church. Among their adventures in that large cosmopolitan city, another vibrant crossroads of the Roman world, was their encounter at the synagogue with a visitor named Apollos, an Alexandrian Jewish Christian. His preaching was eloquent (Acts 18:24–28). He vigorously taught that Jesus was indeed the awaited Messiah. As Prisca and Aquila listened to his proclamation, however, they realized his understanding of baptism was inadequate; he "knew only the baptism of John" (Acts 18:25). That probably meant he had not understood the Christian emphasis on the role of the Spirit in a believer's life. So, Prisca and Aquila "took him aside and explained to him the Way more accurately" (Acts 18:26). Some scholars think that because Prisca's name is often, unconventionally for the time, placed first in references to the couple, that she may have been the more dominant Christian teacher or leader.

Prisca and Aquila did not see Paul again for many years. They may have crossed paths next in the early 60s, when Paul arrived in Rome but not as Paul had planned. Positing that reunion, however, depends on whether they were still alive in Rome in the early 60s. They were alive as late as 58, since Paul greets them in the Letter to the Romans, which he wrote that year. Apparently, the couple had left Ephesus, sensing that Rome was safe enough for Christian believers to return. There, they established another house church. As Paul prepared his lengthy Letter to the Romans to be sent with Phoebe, he sent many greetings to Roman believers, naming his married coworker friends first: "Greet Prisca and Aquila, my co-workers in Christ Jesus, who risked their necks for my life, to whom not only am I grateful but also all the churches of the Gentiles; greet also the church at their house" (Romans 16:3–5).

Silas/Silvanus of Jerusalem

Called Silas in Acts and Silvanus by Paul, this coworker was a Jewish Christian from Jerusalem. Along with a man named Judas Barsabbas, he was chosen after the Council of Jerusalem (Acts 15:22) to accompany Paul and Barnabas back to Antioch. Their assignment was to deliver the letter James had insisted upon sending about the implementation of some Jewish dietary and marriage customs among the Gentile converts. This suggests Silas was positive about the conversion of the Gentiles. When Paul and Barnabas decided not to travel together, Paul chose Silas as his companion. That was an astute move since it linked Paul's work closely with the Jerusalem community.

Silas remained with Paul throughout his travels between 50 and 52, at least as far as Corinth. Along with Paul he was beaten in Philippi (1 Thessalonians 2:1–2) and expelled from Thessalonica, spirited away to Beroea and again attacked there. He eventually caught up with Paul in Corinth. While in Corinth, Paul wrote 1 Thessalonians. He named Silas and their other companion Timothy as coauthors. This reflects that Silas' travels with Paul were closely woven with the presence of Timothy, to whom we will turn next. Nothing further about Silas' association with Paul is known after Paul's time in Corinth ended in 52. It may be that Silas returned to Jerusalem. Some think he is the Silvanus named in 1 Peter 5:12, perhaps as the scribe or the bearer of that missive.

Timothy of Lystra, Son of Eunice, Grandson of Lois

When Paul and Silas left Antioch on what later commentators would say was Paul's second journey, they took the overland route north and northwest through his home region of Tarsus, then through the Taurus mountains into the interior of Galatia. This enabled Paul's desired return to some of the places he and Barnabas had earlier evangelized, Derbe, Lystra, and Iconium (Acts 15:36).

In Lystra, Paul reconnected with Lois, her daughter Eunice, and Eunice's son Timothy, all of whom Paul and Barnabas had apparently known during their time together there. What little can be known about Lois and Eunice is found in Acts and 2 Timothy. It appears that Timothy's conversion came after his mother and grandmother had become believers (2 Timothy 1:5). They were said to have acquainted Timothy from childhood with the "sacred scriptures, which are capable of giving you wisdom for salvation through faith in Christ Jesus" (2 Timothy 3:15).

Acts 16:1 indicates that Eunice was a Jewish woman, as was apparently her mother Lois, and that she had married a Gentile before becoming a Christian. She had not had her son circumcised. Acts 16:2 notes that "the brothers in Lystra and Iconium spoke highly" of Timothy. Hence, Paul wanted Timothy's accompaniment on his missionary travels. Then Acts 16:3 adds a puzzling detail: "On account of the Jews of that region, Paul had him circumcised, for they all knew his father was a Greek." Commentators remain puzzled why Paul had Timothy circumcised, given his strong position against requiring circumcision for Gentile converts. The text implies that, were it not for the surrounding Jews, Paul would not have done this. Was the circumcision to be perceived as a sign that would make Timothy more effective as Paul's coworker among the Jews of his native area and elsewhere? Paul's motive is elusive. In any case, Timothy became one of Paul's extraordinary coworkers and an effective missionary with both Jewish and Gentile Christians.

Timothy accompanied Paul from 50 through 52, the same period Silvanus was also their partner. 1 Thessalonians names the trio as the co-senders of that letter. Timothy is also noted as being with Paul intermittently during the years 54–58. Paul often sent him as an emissary to various churches. He is also named as the co-sender of two letters Paul wrote from prison in those years (Philippians 1:1–13; Philemon 1). Timothy's importance as one of Paul's most significant coworkers is reflected in his being the recipient of the two pastoral letters, 1 and 2 Timothy.

The Pastoral Challenges Paul and His Coworkers Faced

In retrospect, looking at Paul's overall missionary field, we see that he and his coworkers had evangelized both Jews and Gentiles across major sections of the northeastern quadrant of the Mediterranean basin. They had established churches in major cities and seaports such as Ephesus, Athens, Philippi, Thessalonica, and Corinth; they had also preached to groups in many small towns, anywhere an audience of one or more gathered to listen to the Gospel that Paul announced.

Even from afar, Paul guided the groups he had formed, avidly responding to reports he received about them.

Given the frequent negative reactions to Paul's preaching, in some places he managed to stay only a short time, perhaps at best weeks or a few months, to guide the new believers (although he managed to stay in Corinth and Ephesus for longer periods). Often, however, Paul left town sooner than he had planned. While he continuously moved on, meeting more people and forming new cells of believers, it pained him not to remain longer with his new converts nor to easily make return visits to them. His absences caused him to turn to writing letters to maintain his close relationships, to offer pastoral advice, and sometimes to express disappointment with developments in certain groups. Thus, even from afar, Paul guided the groups he had formed, avidly responding to reports he received about them. His correspondence became a form of his apostolic presence among them. While some of those letters have survived and are included in the New Testament, many were likely lost.

Paul's coworkers, evidently of less interest to authorities, could often remain behind the ousted Paul. Also, they more readily made return visits to deliver letters and to continue forming the believers into a worshiping community. They and Paul referred to each of the small cells of believers as an *ekklēsia,* plural, *ekklēsiae.* That Greek term (church in English) signified a gathering of people with a common purpose. It was analogous to the Jewish idea of a *synagōgē,* synagogue, a grouping of believers; the term *synagogue* could also refer to the Jews' building, if they happened to have one (which was rare). As Christianity developed, the word *church* eventually functioned in a parallel manner with its primary sense meaning the group of all believers and its secondary sense the physical building for worship. This distinction is significant in contemporary Catholicism, which has placed renewed emphasis upon the community of believers since the Second Vatican Council, reminding members that all the believers (not just the hierarchy) constitute the Church. The Second Vatican Council document *Lumen gentium* calls the Church the "people of God" (see chapter 6 of *Lumen gentium*).

The main focus of worship, or ritual, in Paul's *ekklēsiae* was the Sabbath meal now infused with Jesus' command at the Last Supper to remember he had promised to be with them in the blessing of the bread and wine. There were probably numerous sociological issues in addition to those earlier noted regarding food sharing and table fellowship. Further, I would guess that marriages that developed between Jewish and Gentile Christian members of a church may have created uncomfortable situations for, say, the Jewish side as it was not used to discarding its dietary laws. Recall that giving up some dietary laws is not that easy; a person who has spent his or her life avoiding a certain food may not want to eat what is served, even when such is not prohibited.

On the sociological level, there were issues of status among believers, with some of the richer hosts giving preference to their friends when it came to food. Paul resolved that type of issue by telling members to eat at home first, leaving only the essential elements of bread and wine as the food at the celebration (see 1 Corinthians 11:20–22).

Who Was Moses? Who Was King David? What Is a Messiah?

Paul's Eucharistic gatherings were a prime occasion for teaching the believers. As more and more Gentiles joined the groups, Paul and his coworkers had the enormous task of explaining the basic beliefs of Judaism upon which the Christian movement and its theological understandings of Jesus' life, death, and resurrection were premised. The Gentiles who believed God had raised Jesus and whom Paul welcomed into the churches he established, except for those who had been God-fearers, did not share a common background of religious knowledge with the Jewish Christians.

Imagine Paul's situation: The Gentiles had not been waiting for a messiah! And they would logically have wondered, Why does it matter that Jesus was a descendant of the ancient King David? What is a messiah? Most also would have known nothing of Abraham and Moses, the Ten Commandments, the prophets, the psalms, and the myriad of Jewish laws and customs. Nor would they have understood how fundamental the Passover celebration and theology of redemption was to the Jews and to Jesus himself.

As the Gentiles became Christians, they comprehended that God had raised the crucified Jesus from the dead and that God's power over death could be extended to anyone who followed Christ and his ways. Belief in the saving death of Christ and his resurrection was the cornerstone upon which Paul could proceed to expand their religious development. Throughout his letters, Paul's profound theological explanations can be seen. Since Paul's letters are occasional, though, it is not always easy to systematize his thought into logically stated reasoning—that is, usually he was responding to specific problems or controversies within the churches. As much as we might wish, he did not write treatises on such topics as the theology of redemption or the theology of the Eucharist. Usually, Paul wrote to answer questions the believers had raised or to respond to reports he had heard about them. Sometimes he was encouraging, but other times he was critical and upset at negative developments in a church. To complicate matters further, as we read Paul's letters, which answer questions or offer advice on dilemmas, we are in the dark when it comes to the details. Reading only one side of a correspondence can be difficult.

Paul's Letter to the Romans, however, has a systematic approach. When Paul penned that letter to send along with Phoebe, he was in Corinth preparing to visit Rome and the believers there for the first time. Not only did he intend for the letter to introduce him to the community but for it to lay out the heart of his teaching. (He had anticipated that negative reports about him by his various opponents, for example, those he dubbed "superapostles" [2 Corinthians 11:5], would precede him.) Yet even this extraordinary document does not offer a complete compilation of his vast and detailed teaching.

Paul the Theologian

Paul's background as a Pharisee and his upbringing and early education as a Hellenistic Jew amid Gentile culture prepared him to convey Jewish Christian thought about Jesus to non-Jewish listeners. His linguistic abilities and multicultural understanding were notable strengths. Even more than communicating his Jewish Christian thought to Gentiles, Paul had to formulate the theological language his Gentile converts would comprehend. He drew upon many creative metaphors to explain himself, such as the baptismal imagery of dying and rising. Additionally, along with communicating theological concepts, Paul needed to counter the complexity of Greco-Roman religious beliefs, complete with gods and goddesses, that had been part of the culture of the Gentiles for centuries. In other words, Paul had the challenging task of leading the new believers in Christ from polytheism into monotheism.

Paul was able to recognize those who were sincere converts. They were the ones who had genuinely "turned to God from idols to serve the living and true God" (1 Thessalonians 1:9); they had accepted his teaching, the Gospel, as it came to them "in power and in the holy Spirit and [with] much conviction" (1 Thessalonians 1:5). Paul observed in them "joy from the holy Spirit" as they responded to the Gospel (1 Thessalonians 1:6).

It would be naïve to think that Gentile converts transitioned into Paul's groups of believers, however, without social or economic consequences. Nor should we assume that no one returned to their prior beliefs. Such recidivism would not be surprising. To become one of the few monotheists in societies whose cultures, including frequent public celebrations, were imbued with polytheism was for a new convert to deny what most other people—that is, family, friends, employers, customers—thought was important. No wonder Paul observed, as quoted earlier, that the Spirit came to them "with much conviction." They needed that undergirding to survive socially.

Besides the most basic Hebrew teachings on monotheism, Paul also had to explain profound theological concepts such as the need for redemption from sin and the need for reconciliation with God through the sacrifice, death, and resurrection of Jesus. Likewise, Paul needed to help his converts understand that in their baptismal choice to die to sin and unite themselves with Jesus, they had been made righteous. This meant they had experienced justification before God by the grace of God and hence were living as a new creation (2 Corinthians 5:17), as adopted children of God (Romans 8:15). Paul's theological teaching was reflected liturgically when those who gathered celebrated their transformation into redeemed sons and daughters of God, reconciled to God through their choice to follow Jesus (2 Corinthians 5:18).

A Brief Case Study of the Earliest Female Believers in Thessalonica

With their new Gentile converts, Paul and his coworkers were arguing against centuries of long-established beliefs—beliefs bolstered by an impressive pantheon of Greco-Roman and other local gods and goddesses and even imported cults from places such as Egypt. Beliefs and customs regarding these deities pervaded the cultural world in which the Gentiles lived and anchored their religious lives and cultural matrix. As an example of the complexities involved in turning away from the old deities—for both those preaching and the new believers in Christ—I will turn briefly to the situation of the very earliest female converts in Thessalonica.

Paul's First Letter to the Thessalonians, his earliest extant letter, was written only a few months after he, Silvanus, and Timothy had first been in that city in 49. What we read in that epistle about the believers in that place is the closest temporal record we have about new converts. I have become especially interested in the female believers in Thessalonica and how conversion impacted their lives regarding childbirth.

Giving birth in the ancient world was fraught with dangers for both mother and child. Infant and maternal mortality statistics were high. Practices imploring the help of various goddesses, incantations to be recited by midwives, the use of amulets, herbs, and statuettes for mothers, and pre- and postnatal visits to shrines had developed over centuries. Women depended on their accumulated observations and midwives to know which practices were helpful.

What if you were a newly Christian woman, pregnant, and rightfully fearful of childbirth? A conversion to monotheism, belief in Jesus, meant jettisoning belief in all other gods and goddesses. Whom should you call upon now? Jesus, the Father, the Spirit? Of course, but did they understand your fears as female goddesses supposedly had? And what if your midwife pressed upon you to hold in your hand a goddess' amulet as you labored? What if your mother, aunts, sisters, and girlfriends said that a certain goddess had helped them give birth? How easy was it to leave behind women's accumulated wisdom—that is, what others had said were the tried-and-true helper deities?

This hypothetical situation suggests why a relapse into some of the former beliefs would not have been surprising. It also indicates that Paul needed a solution. He could not just deny the existence of the traditional deities; he needed to replace them. In my estimation, 1 Thessalonians 2:7 offers a clue in the strange female metaphor Paul uses to describe the attitude possessed when he, Timothy, and Silvanus were with the Thessalonians: "We were gentle among you, as a nursing mother cares for her children." In recent studies,[3] I have theorized that this singular female metaphor comparing three men to one nursing mother was part of Paul's attempt to erase the old goddesses. Paul was the nursing mother now, and with his two helpers offered the sustenance of the Gospel.[4]

Recent archaeological excavations in Thessalonica have found evidence of a nursing goddess' shrine that functioned in Paul's time. This may have been the location of worship of the type of local goddess against whom Paul needed to compete. Also, in the broader region of Thessalonica, archaeology has recovered evidence of nursing goddesses portrayed as a threesome, one goddess with two assistants. Were there amulets or shrines Paul's Christian women had known that portrayed such a trio? Now Paul and his two helpers had replaced them.

This is just one example of how difficult conversion must have been both for the earliest new believers and the evangelizers who had to help them abandon their religious past. Of course, as the numbers

3. See Florence Morgan Gillman, "Paul, His Nurse Metaphor (1 Thessalonians 2:7) and the Thessalonian Women Who Turned against Their Idols," *Catholic Biblical Quarterly* 84, 2 (2022), 279–294; Gillman, 1 Thessalonians, 41–56.

4. Paul uses the imagery of giving his converts milk also in 1 Corinthians 3:2, but he does not refer to doing so as a nursing mother.

in a Christian group increased, the social support for the transition to monotheism would have grown likewise.

The Opponents and the Superapostles

Paul's extensive missionary work had truly made him the apostle to the Gentiles, as Jesus is said to have commissioned him in the event on the road to Damascus. Paul was not, however, the only person proclaiming the resurrection of Christ throughout the same regions. Barnabas also remained a missionary, whose teaching we presume continued to accord with Paul's, although the details of his later life and work are unknown. And traditions abound about the missionary work of the twelve. One could guess that, undoubtedly, conflicts could arise on many issues—which they did. Paul himself experienced much of this.

From the Letter to the Galatians, for example, we learn that there were subsequent visitors to Paul's churches who contradicted him and decried his teaching as incomplete or in need of correction. These intruders told the Galatians, contrary to the decision of the Council of Jerusalem, that male circumcision was necessary for Gentile Christian men. When Paul got wind of that development, he wrote the scathing Letter to the Galatians. Paul's fury as he wrote is evidenced by his omission of the traditional thanksgiving with which a writer of his time would normally begin such correspondence. (Such a thanksgiving is found in the rest of Paul's letters.) Furthermore, he berated the Galatians for following "a different gospel" (Galatians 1:6) rather than "the one we [Paul and his coworkers] preached to you" (Galatians 1:8). Paul's harsh critique was against the Galatians' acceptance that the act of circumcision was necessary for their salvation, meaning that faith in Christ was itself insufficient for one's salvation. Paul's sharp comment about the other preachers who had misled the Galatians was an acerbic barb: "Would that those who are upsetting you might also castrate themselves" (Galatians 5:12).

"His bodily presence is weak" (2 Corinthians 10:10)

From 2 Corinthians, we learn that some preachers who had visited Paul's congregation in Corinth critiqued his personality and his demeanor. He quotes them as saying, "his [Paul's] letters are severe and forceful, but his bodily presence is weak, and his speech contemptible" (2 Corinthians 10:10). Paul's response was that those agitators were "boasting beyond measure in other people's [his] labors" (10:15). He scornfully dubbed them "superapostles" and offered this defense: "Even if I am untrained in speaking, I am not so in knowledge" (2 Corinthians 11:5–6).

Elsewhere in Paul's letters, there is evidence of other slights lodged against him and his appearance. Therefore, it is an irony of history—or, better said from Paul's framework, the work of the Spirit—that it is the forceful preaching conveyed in his powerful letter writing, not the eloquence of the apparently handsome superapostles, that has survived the ages and continues to inspire our belief.

Boldness in Action and Speech

Bitter attacks against Paul forced him to come to the defense of his ministry. He did so with warfare imagery (2 Corinthians 10:4). His intended response to those who accused him of "acting according to the flesh"—that is, according to human standards (for personal gain)—was to "act boldly" against them (2 Corinthians 10:2). This he did from a distance most powerfully through his writing, but he indicated he would not hesitate to argue in person as well: "What we are in word through letters when absent, that we also are when present" (2 Corinthians 10:11). These statements from Paul raise the subject of his boldness in both action and speech. There are several indications in his letters where he comments on his courageous speech and action. The Greek term for boldness that he sometimes used is *parrēsia*.

To cite a few examples, in 2 Corinthians 3:12–17, Paul declares that his ministry in the Spirit is more glorious and enduring than that of Moses, asserting: "Since we have such hope, we act very boldly and not like Moses, who put a veil over his face so that the Israelites could not look intently at the cessation of what was fading [the glory that shone on his face]." Elsewhere, in 1 Thessalonians 2:2 Paul similarly states: "After we had suffered and been insolently treated . . . in Philippi, we drew courage [literally: boldly proclaimed] through our God to speak to you the gospel of God." It is evident that Paul's sense of boldness came from his conviction that his ministry was from God. Likewise, a sense of endurance bolstered the conviction as Paul successfully weathered the dangers of his ministry.

Paul's sense of boldness came from his conviction that his ministry was from God.

This concept of *parrēsia* was a matter primarily for academic discussion until Francis' papacy. He has used *parrēsia* (also written *parrhesía*) in various public addresses. For example, in the apostolic exhortation *Evangelii gaudium* (*The Joy of the Gospel*), he named the Holy Spirit as the source for "the courage to proclaim the newness of the Gospel with boldness (*parrhesía*) in every time and place, even when it meets with opposition."[5] In a later apostolic exhortation *Gaudete et exsultate* (*Rejoice and Be Glad*) Francis defines *parrhesía* specifically as "apostolic fervour," expressed as "an impulse to evangelize and to leave a mark in this world."[6]

The Conventional Iconography of Paul

The superapostles' insult regarding Paul's appearance raises the question of what he looked like, although there is no certain data about that. Besides the superapostles' alleging that Paul's bodily presence was weak (whatever that meant?), Paul referred to a problem

5. *Evangelii gaudium*, 259.

6. *Gaudete et exsultate*, 129.

with his eyes. Was this disfiguring? In Galatians 4:13–15, Paul states: "You know that it was because of a physical illness that I originally preached the gospel to you, and you did not show disdain or contempt because of the trial caused you by my physical condition . . . If it had been possible, you would have torn out your eyes and given them to me." Was this actually about his eyes or was he emphasizing the extent to which they were willing to help him? Was his illness an ongoing and unpleasant condition? Many think it was indeed an eye problem, since he also commented in the same letter, rather triumphantly as if he had improved, that he was writing to them in "large letters" and "in my own hand" (6:11).

Another allusion to Paul's appearance may be his comment in 2 Corinthians 12:7 that he had been given (by God?) "a thorn in the flesh." This may have referred to a physical disability or handicap, although it could also be a figurative way of denoting a personal temptation or a troublesome opponent.

Much of the art depicting Paul draws upon a literary description of him that is found in a late second-century apocryphal document titled the Acts of Paul and Thecla. There, Paul is described as "a man small of stature, with a bald head and crooked legs, in a good state of body, with eyebrows meeting and nose somewhat hooked, full of friendliness; for now he appeared like a man, and now he had the face of an angel."[7] The accuracy of this description, written more than a century and a half after Paul's death, cannot be verified although it is possible some memory of his appearance survived more than a hundred and fifty years. On the other hand, a century and a half can also be seen as too long a gap for any such dependable information. In either case, this literary sketch of Paul has become the basis for many artists' portrayals of him. The depiction of Paul arriving in Neapolis on this book's cover reflects the traditional description of him.

7. E. Hennecke, *New Testament Apocrypha*. vol. 2; ed. W. Schneemelcher (Tübingen: Mohr 1964), 354.

More recently, in 2009, a fresco of Paul dating to about 380 was found in Rome in the catacomb of St. Thekla, about a third of a mile from the basilica built over his traditional burial spot, St. Paul Outside-the-Walls. This catacomb was discovered only by chance in 1950 during construction of an office building. The painting of Paul, together with images of Peter, Andrew, and John, was found on the ceiling of the burial chamber of a Roman noblewoman who had commissioned artists to decorate it with biblical scenes. The four paintings are found in arches surrounding an image of the Good Shepherd. This oldest extant portrayal of Paul reflects the iconographic characteristics described of a thin face and dark beard.

Chapter 6

Paul's Later Years and Death

Before discussing our experience of Paul's letters proclaimed from the lectionary in the liturgy today, it is important to consider his later years and what is known about his death. First, some key dates in his life will be summarized, with the realization that most dates in Pauline chronology are approximations, and that an ongoing debate among scholars continues to refine those dates.

In my estimation, which parallels that of many other scholars, and as I have outlined in these pages so far, the event on the road to Damascus took place in about 37, followed by three years in Arabia (37–40), ending with a brief visit to Jerusalem in 40. From 40 to 45 Paul was back in Tarsus, then recruited by Barnabas to help him in Antioch in 45. The first journey of Paul and Barnabas was from 46 to 49, followed by the Council of Jerusalem in 50. The second and third journeys of Paul with his other companions date respectively to approximately 50–52 and 53–58.

In Corinth in the year 58, Paul wrote to the Romans, alerting them of his plans to visit while on his way to preach in Spain. Prior to traveling to Rome, however, Paul needed to return to Jerusalem to deliver money raised from mainly Gentile churches for the famine-stricken poor. Once that mission was completed, he could easily get passage from the Judean port of Caesarea for Rome, likely traveling on one of the frequent grain ships transporting food from Egypt to the Roman metropolis.

The Best-Laid Plans

Paul indeed left Corinth and, by way of one last visit to the region of Ephesus, he journeyed to Jerusalem. He still intended to depart from Caesarea for Rome, but this did not work out as smoothly as he had planned. (In Acts 21–28, Luke reports the traditions he had learned about this Jerusalem-Caesarea-Rome period, dating from between about 58 and 62.)

The radical changes to Paul's plans came about during his stay in Jerusalem. He seems to have delivered the collection safely. And he must have been pleased that its acceptance by the Jewish Christians of Jerusalem signaled that they recognized the Gentile Christian donors as their brothers and sisters in Christ. Their acceptance would have further indicated that they approved of Paul's mission to the Gentiles. Nevertheless, controversy arose alleging that he had taken an uncircumcised Gentile male named Trophimus, from Ephesus, with him into the temple court reserved for Jewish men (Acts 21:27–29). An uproar over this resulted in Paul's arrest and appearance before the Sanhedrin.

Just over three decades earlier, Paul and his teacher Gamaliel had been well known among Jerusalem Pharisees, and Gamaliel himself was a member of the Sanhedrin. Now, with Gamaliel presumably dead (since he is not mentioned),[1] Paul relied upon other Pharisees who, at least theologically, came to his defense regarding his preaching of the resurrection. But the temple allegation was so serious in conservative Jerusalem that Paul was put under protective arrest. After some days, he was transferred to the Roman Procurator (Governor) Felix in Caesarea to be put on trial there. Unfortunately for Paul, Felix was in no rush to conduct his trial, probably because he was thinking Paul might bribe him. Had Felix heard rumors, confused by talk about Paul's collection, that Paul

"This man is doing nothing that deserves death or imprisonment." (Acts 26:31)

1. Various traditions outside the Bible place his death in about 52.

had brought a lot of money to Jerusalem? This resulted in Paul being left in prison from 58 until 60—that is, until Felix's term in office ended and the arrival of the new procurator, Festus.

Festus wasted little time in scheduling Paul's trial, which included an interview with the visiting tetrarch of Galilee and Peraea, Herod Agrippa I, and his sister-consort, Berenice. Paul's trial, at which he recounted his experience on the road to Damascus, resulted in the governor and the royal pair deciding, "This man is doing nothing that deserves death or imprisonment" (Acts 26:31). Were they frightened by Paul's forceful witness in his preaching of the resurrection? Paul might have been freed then, except that he demanded implementation of his right, as a Roman citizen, to be tried in Rome. Thus, Paul was sent to Italy as a prisoner in the custody of a Roman centurion named Julius.

In Acts 27:1—28:13, Luke's account of Paul's dangerous sea journey consists of one of the most detailed extant reports of an ancient sea journey in the eastern Mediterranean.

"He remained there for two full years in his lodgings" (Acts 28:30)

After spending the winter in Malta, a period that included healing Publius, the father of the chief man of the island, Paul and his centurion sailed to Syracuse in Sicily, then Rhegium, and finally disembarked at the important Roman seaport of Puteoli. During their seven-day stay, word of their arrival preceded them to Rome. Some Roman Christians came out to meet them as they approached the city near the Forum of Appius and Three Taverns. Perhaps Prisca and Aquila, who, as of 58, hosted a house church in Rome, were among those greeting Paul in 60. Luke states that upon seeing the Roman Christians, "Paul gave thanks to God and took courage" (Acts 28:15). Luke also notes that Paul was allowed to live by himself, although he was guarded by a Roman soldier. Paul, of course, proceeded immediately to preach to all who came to listen.

Luke concludes his narrative about Paul's arrival in Rome rather strangely (Acts 28:30–31). He simply observes that Paul remained there two years, presumably under house arrest within his own lodgings, and that he could teach about Jesus to all who came to hear. With that information Luke's text abruptly ends. Surely Luke, writing around 90, must have known what happened to Paul in Rome in 62 and thereafter. Why does he not tell us?

Were the last parts of Luke's manuscript of Acts lost? Or was he more concerned with concluding his narrative with Paul preaching in Rome, the capital and administrative center of the empire? And, on an even wider level, was Luke concluding his two-volume work by showing that the Jesus movement, which had begun in Galilee among the rural Jewish people, was then within only decades of being preached to the Gentile Roman urbanites? Other than these possible suggestions, there is no satisfactory explanation of why Luke ends Acts as he does.

There is also no indisputable evidence of what happened to Paul immediately after his imprisonment ended in 62. Some theorize he traveled as far as Spain, as he had once planned (Romans 15:24). Whatever he did, the strongest traditions about his final years place him still in or back in Rome during the years of the Neronian persecution between 64 and 67.

I like to imagine days that Paul sat with Prisca and Aquila by the banks of the Tiber, reminiscing about their travels and the converts who came to their house churches, many of whom they may have baptized in the murky waters of that river. The three must have wondered about the future for the believers in Christ. Did they have any idea of how foundational their faith had been for so many?

Paul's Death and Burial

Rome had undergone a massive, devastating fire in 64 and, searching for a scapegoat, Emperor Nero blamed the Christians. This resulted in the persecution and death of many Christians, perhaps including Prisca and Aquila if they were still alive. According to early Church traditions, both Peter and Paul were in Rome then, and both are thought to have been martyred during that persecution. Peter was crucified upside down in Nero's circus and Paul was beheaded outside the walls of Rome at the spot known as Tre Fontane (Three Fountains) on the Via Ostiensis. Paul was then buried further along that route on an estate owned by a Christian woman, Lucina.

In the fourth century, Emperor Constantine erected a church over Paul's grave. Later emperors adapted and enlarged the church. After a fire destroyed it in 1823, the building was reconstructed and is known as the Papal Basilica of St. Paul Outside-the-Walls.[2] Under the main altar, owing to recent excavations, is situated a marble sarcophagus about eight feet long, with the inscription PAULO APOSTOLO MART (Paul Apostle Martyr). The site was excavated because pilgrims visiting Rome in 2000 for the Catholic Church's Jubilee celebration registered great disappointment that Paul's tomb, buried under layers of plaster and unreachable because of an iron gate, could not be well seen or visited.

In 2002, Vatican archaeologists undertook an excavation. The top of the sarcophagus contained numerous small holes, owing to the practice of ancient pilgrims' lowering cloth into a saint's grave to try to touch the person's remains. The inside of the tomb was examined by endoscopy and showed pieces of purple and blue linen and some bone fragments. DNA testing, to the disappointment of many, was not done, but may still occur in the future. The bone fragments date to the first or second century, thus supporting the probability of Paul's burial there. On June 28, 2009, Pope Benedict XVI stated that the dating of the bones "seems to confirm the unanimous and undisputed tradition according to which these are the mortal remains of the Apostle Paul."[3]

---

2. "The Tomb of the Apostle," accessed June 16, 2022, https://www.vatican.va/various/basiliche/san_paolo/en/basilica/tomba.htm.

3. "Pope says relics are those of St. Paul," Religion News Service, accessed June 8, 2022, https://religionnews.com/2009/06/30/pope-says-relics-are-those-of-st-paul/.

Under the Threat of Persecution

The burials of martyrs such as Paul are difficult to analyze since early Christians, for the sake of protecting martyrs' remains, occasionally moved their bones and later reburied them. For example, in Paul's case, there is a tradition that both his remains and those of Peter were for a time in the mid-third century moved for safeguarding into the catacombs beneath San Sebastiano on the Via Appia. This relocation would have been during the persecutions carried on by Emperor Valerianus between 257 and 258. Tradition holds that Paul's remains were later returned to St. Paul Outside-the-Walls and Peter's were placed beneath the Vatican. This removal and reburial could explain why the recent excavation found that the bones thought to be Paul's had been wrapped in purple cloth, a sign of great respect. To add even further to these complicated traditions, it is also claimed that the heads of St. Paul and St. Peter are in the Basilica of St. John Lateran in Rome. Often, early Christians separated the heads of martyrs from the rest of their remains to extend the accessibility of the martyr's remains to pilgrims. The head of a martyr also enhanced the status of the church that possessed it.

Paul's sarcophagus, lying beneath St. Paul Outside-the-Walls, is a peaceful place for pilgrims to visit and ponder the life of this amazing apostle. Given the probability that Paul's remains are there, and yet even if not, the basilica allows one to feel immersed as one more soul in the great band of all those Christian believers, that "great cloud of witnesses" (Hebrews 12:1), for whom over the centuries his life and teaching have made a difference.

St. Paul Outside-the-Walls is a long way from Jerusalem and the road to Damascus. Paul must have looked back many times in his life to his decision to start out for Damascus. What a steppingstone that route became. How interesting that the road led to Rome.

CHAPTER 7

The Legacy of Paul's Letters

None of the papyri on which Paul wrote still exists, but fortunately for Christianity, early believers copied Paul's letters. Still, it is assumed that Paul wrote many more letters than those preserved in the Bible. In fact, Paul's letters refer to others. In 1 and 2 Corinthians (1 Corinthians 5:9; 2 Corinthians 2:3–4a), for example, Paul mentions two other letters to the community. Paul also indicates in the Letter to the Ephesians (3:3) that an earlier letter had been written to that church. Finally, his Letter to the Colossians (4:16) cites a letter that he wrote to the Laodiceans. The many epistles that have survived and were repeatedly copied are simply invaluable; they communicate Paul's activities, struggles, hopes, his theological thought, his and his churches' problems, arguments, and the spirit Paul possessed. What treasures!

It is evident that certain letters circulated widely. Paul himself told his churches to pass around some letters (Colossians 4:16). His epistles also moved quickly through the wider Mediterranean region. For example, around 95, the apostolic Father of the Church, Bishop Clement, of Rome, wrote a letter to the Corinthian church (1 Clement) in which he referred to a letter (that is, 1 Corinthians) that Paul had written to them (1 Clement 47:2–4). By Clement's time, then, Paul's letter was known in Rome. Since Clement wrote from the generation after the apostles, his lengthy and interesting letter is not included in the New Testament. Also, in the latter years of the first century and the beginning of the second, there is evidence that the collection of many Pauline writings was underway. The study of these documents —that is, the manuscript history of Paul's letters—is an important area of biblical studies that involves examining both the writing of the text and the material upon which it is written.

Will More Epistles by Paul Be Found?

There is always hope that additional epistles and older copies of the ones that the Church possesses will be found. Where might that be? As with the discovery of many ancient manuscripts related to the Old Testament, such as the Dead Sea Scrolls first discovered in 1947, the conditions most likely to have allowed for preservation are desert areas with low humidity. Ancient monasteries and desert caves, but surprisingly also the long-buried ancient dumps of Egypt, such as in the Fayum region, hold out much hope. Scholars are always on the alert for new discoveries coming from the painstaking work of archaeologists.

Scholars are always on the alert for new discoveries coming from the painstaking work of archaeologists.

One of the greatest complications in comparing old manuscripts is that ancient copyists sometimes misspelled or left out words or even whole lines. Yet more challenging is that occasionally, contrary to the rules of their trade, and because some had their own agendas, scribes added or omitted phrases intentionally. Biblical scholars, called textual critics, specialize in sorting out the changes, omissions, and additions in the manuscripts that have survived. The most significant variations in the texts are usually discussed in biblical footnotes.

The oldest extant but incomplete manuscript of Paul's epistles is Papyrus 46, dated between 175 and 225. Written in codex (book, not scroll) form, its origin is unknown. It was most likely found somewhere in Egypt, perhaps in an ancient monastery. Some of its pages first came to light in the 1930s, when a Cairo antiquities dealer offered some leaves for sale. Unfortunately, the whole manuscript was broken apart and gradually sold in batches. The University of Michigan and the Chester Beatty Collection, Dublin, Ireland, purchased all the known leaves.

"I, Tertius, the writer of this letter . . ." (Romans 16:22)

While Paul was a skilled writer, as a person of his times he would have normally dictated his letters to a scribe, an *amanuensis*. One can almost envision Paul pacing up and down or absent-mindedly sewing tents as he formulated his thoughts and dictated them to a scribe sitting nearby. Scribes, who could be men or women, were skilled letter writers who made a living at their trade. In Romans (16:22), Paul's scribe Tertius addresses the community: "I, Tertius, the writer of this letter, greet you [the Romans] in the Lord." Did the Roman believers already know the scribe somehow, from other letters, or was he trying to establish a bond he would have with them if he traveled to Rome with Paul? Some scribes were so trusted that they did not merely take dictation but could be instructed to craft a paragraph or more of the writer's thought. During Paul's various periods in Corinth, Prisca may have been one of his scribes.

The Pauline Corpus

Over the centuries, thirteen of the twenty-seven epistles in the New Testament have been attributed to Paul. They form what is called the Pauline corpus.[1] Since the late eighteenth and early nineteenth centuries, with the rise of modern historical biblical criticism (analysis), scholars have made various distinctions among these. They grouped some together and separated out others as more likely having been attributed to Paul than written by him. It is interesting to observe these distinctions and to see some of the implications of why this is important. Scholars have studied the grammar, vocabulary, structural characteristics, theological terms and concepts, and consistency of reasoning, to name just some of the types of analysis scholarship has applied to the Pauline corpus.

1. The Letter to the Hebrews has sometimes been considered a fourteenth letter in the Pauline corpus, but since there is no evidence that it is related to Paul, that connection has been set aside.

While there is not an absolute consensus, widespread agreement exists that seven of the Pauline letters are by Paul. These are called the authentic letters and consist of Romans, 1 and 2 Corinthians, Galatians, Philippians, Philemon, and 1 Thessalonians.

The six other letters, called the deutero-Paulines, are Ephesians, Colossians, 2 Thessalonians, 1 and 2 Timothy, and Titus. The Greek term *deutero* means secondary. This is an important distinction because it implies these documents are indeed Pauline, but reasons exist to question whether Paul is the author. Nevertheless, the letters belong to the Pauline corpus, and the Church has always regarded them as inspired Scripture.

To summarize in two points what could otherwise be a long and painstaking analysis: First, there is rather general agreement that 1 and 2 Timothy and Titus were written by someone who was influenced by Paul but lived a generation or two after him. Those three letters form a group known as the pastorals. Second, there remains much intense debate about Paul's authorship of Ephesians, Colossians, and 2 Thessalonians. Many strongly defend Paul's authorship of some or all of these, while others continue to raise serious doubts. (Because the arguments are so compelling both for and against Paul's authorship of these latter three epistles, I remain open to the ongoing discussion.)

Regarding the pastorals—1 and 2 Timothy, and Titus—the author's identification of himself as Paul (1 Timothy 1:1; 2 Timothy 1:1; Titus 1:1) appears to be an impersonation. A conclusion should not be reached, however, about the integrity of an author who uses another's name. At that time, it was acceptable to write in another's name, especially if that person had been famous, authoritative, and respected. Some ancient writers were thus rather self-effacing. They cared about their words being taken seriously, and that could mean using an authoritative person's name. Of course, normally the person whose name was used would be deceased so that the letter would not be disowned.

Several letters in the Pauline corpus are also grouped under the captivity or prison letters. This grouping consists of Philippians, Philemon, Colossians, and Ephesians. It is known from Acts that Paul endured various imprisonments: he was jailed in Philippi (Acts 16:16–40), in Caesarea (Acts 23:12—24:27), and in Rome, where he remained for two years under house arrest (Acts 28:16, 30). Although not reported in the epistles or Acts, Paul may have been imprisoned in Rome once again in the years following his release from house arrest.

Even before his Roman incarceration(s), Paul had referred to the "beatings, imprisonments, [and] riots" (2 Corinthians 6:5) he had been through and once, in boasting response to the superapostles, he stated that he had endured "far more imprisonments, far worse beatings and numerous brushes with death" than had his opponents (2 Corinthians 11:23). Luke devotes almost one fourth of Acts to Paul's imprisonment, demonstrating that even as a prisoner Paul sought to advance the preaching of the Gospel (Acts 21:33—28:31). He testified about Christ before magistrates, authorities, and judges, and from them commanded respect. As we comment briefly on the captivity epistles an interesting question to ask is whether those letters are distinctive because Paul wrote them as a prisoner.

Roman prison conditions are known to have been dismal; the quarters were dark, damp, filthy, overcrowded, and unventilated. Prisoners received pitiful amounts of food and water; they were often restrained by chains. Yet a more recent study has observed that in the prison letters Paul does not dwell on his awful conditions:

> Although he names them, surprisingly Paul himself does not bemoan the hardships he faces. Rather, through tact and clarity, he manifests a spirit of joy and freely asserts the preeminence of God's grace. He expands with cosmic dimensions his view of Christ and underscores the universal scope of the ekklesia. . . . With the Philippians he rejoices (Philippians 4:4–10), and with the Colossians, even rejoices in his sufferings (Colossians 1:24); from Philemon, he experienced "much joy

and encouragement" (Philemon 7), and to the Ephesians, he reiterates throughout a message of love, grace and peace.[2]

Chronology within the Pauline Corpus

The order in which Paul's letters were written is important to establish since they help us trace the history of his ministry and show us how his thought developed over time. While scholars are always attempting to refine our knowledge, currently, the sequence[3] is considered to be as follows:

1. 1 Thessalonians is the earliest letter we have; Paul wrote it in about 50, while he was in Corinth after receiving a report about the Thessalonians from Timothy. It is unlikely that this is Paul's first letter to one of his groups since he had been evangelizing since the mid-to-late 30s, but nothing written earlier is extant.

2. Galatians was written about 53, probably from Ephesus while Paul was living there for about two years. Since Galatia is a region, there is much debate about which local churches the letter addresses. The churches may have included those of Derbe, Lystra, and Iconium, which Paul and Barnabas had established in about 50.

3. 1 Corinthians also comes from Ephesus in about 53. It was Paul's second letter to the Corinthians; his earlier letter to them has not survived.

4. Philippians dates to about 55 and seems, likewise, to come from Ephesus; Paul appears to have been in prison when he wrote this missive (Philippians 1:12–13).

5. Philemon also indicates Paul was in prison, perhaps in Ephesus, but some think Rome was more likely. If the letter had been written from Ephesus, it could be dated about 55, but

---

2. See John Gillman, "Paul's Voice Still Resounds in His Letters from Prison," *Word and World* 38, 4 (2018), 345–354, 346–347.

3. See this sequence as similarly laid out by Donald Senior, *Composing Sacred Scripture: How the Bible Was Formed* (Chicago: Liturgy Training Publications, 2016), 55–56.

if it had been written from Rome, it would be much later, sometime in the early 60s.

6. 2 Corinthians fits the time frame between 55 and 56, when Paul was still in Ephesus. It is the fourth letter in the Corinthian correspondence, the third of which is lost (that is, our 1 and 2 Corinthians are actually letters 2 and 4 of a four-part letter exchange). Understanding this letter is complicated by a question of literary integrity—that is whether the length of the letter as we have it was original— since many scholars think it to be a document pieced together from two or more of Paul's letters.

7. Romans, a very long letter laying out much of Paul's teaching, was written from Corinth in 57 or 58 as Paul was making future plans to travel to Rome after first visiting Jerusalem to deliver the collection he had taken up from the Gentile churches for the Jewish Christians.

Since Ephesians, Colossians, and 2 Thessalonians are of disputed authenticity, dating them depends upon what a scholar thinks about their authorship. The pastoral letters—1 and 2 Timothy, and Titus—would obviously have been written after Paul's death in the mid-60s, but how far after cannot be assessed with any certainty.

Paul and Women

In making the distinctions between Paul's authentic letters and the deutero-Pauline epistles, it is logical to discuss Paul's reputation regarding women. Until well into the twentieth century, Paul was cast as being sexist. His statements supporting that characterization come primarily from two sources: the pastoral letters and one of his authentic letters, 1 Corinthians.

To cite some examples, in giving pastoral counsel to Timothy the author of 1 Timothy states:

> Women should adorn themselves with proper conduct, with modesty and self-control, not with braided hairstyles and gold ornaments, or pearls, or expensive clothes, but rather, as befits women who profess

> reverence for God, with good deeds. A woman must receive instruction silently and under complete control, I do not permit a woman to teach or to have authority over a man. She must be quiet. For Adam was formed first, then Eve. Further, Adam was not deceived but the woman was deceived and transgressed. But she will be saved through motherhood, provided women persevere in faith and love and holiness, with self-control. (2:9–15)

In that same letter, "Paul" wrote regarding younger unmarried widows:

> They learn to be idlers going about from house to house, and not only idlers but gossips and busybodies as well, talking about things that should not be mentioned. So I would like younger widows to marry, have children and manage a home, so as to give the adversary no pretext for maligning us. For some have already turned away to follow Satan. (5:13–15).

In the Letter to Titus, "Paul" counseled:

> Older men should be temperate, dignified, self-controlled, sound in faith, love, and endurance. Similarly, older women should be reverent in their behavior, not slanderers, not addicted to drink, teaching what is good so that they may train younger women to love their husbands and children, to be self-controlled, chaste, good homemakers, under the control of their husbands. (2:2–5)

In these three quotes alone, extraordinary limitations on women were being recommended: receiving instructions silently, no teaching, no authority over a man, salvation by motherhood, widows being required to remarry, and women expected to be always controlled by a husband. No wonder some modern biblical readers have looked askance at "Paul."

In this context of discussing which letters Paul wrote, however, it becomes clear that the sexist recommendations come from a later period than Paul's. If that is the case, he cannot be blamed for these statements. Furthermore, they are contradicted by Paul's practice as reflected in his authentic epistles and Acts. As we have earlier observed, he collaborated with many women. Recall that he expressed great appreciation for Phoebe as a deacon and Prisca as his coworker and a house church leader. Further, in 1 Corinthians 7, we have seen that he recommended celibacy to any believer, unmarried or widowed, as he had at that time chosen for himself. That would certainly include, unlike 1 Timothy, widows who chose to remain single as well as women who chose not to ever marry.

Limitations Paul Did Not Set

In this discussion, one can see the importance of the analysis of authorship. Since scholars have widely concluded that Paul did not author 1 Timothy and Titus, the sexism therein cannot be attributed to him. These views are to be ascribed to a later period. This now raises further questions: Why were the author(s) of these letters encouraging strict patriarchal limitations on women? Why were they changing Christianity's earlier egalitarianism as seen in Paul's praxis? Since the answer to these questions involves the post-Pauline historical period, which is beyond our purview here, only a few points will be made.

While the unknown author(s) of the pastorals must have moved enough in Pauline circles to have a sense of what Paul was like and how letters from him might sound, in their later period Christians faced new issues. In the latter decades of the first century, given the growth in numbers of believers, Roman society more heavily scrutinized Christian social praxis. The Romans did not necessarily like what they saw. While many Christians, including Paul, had died in the mid-60s in the Neronian persecution, increasingly on a wider level Christians experienced a range of social problems. For example, they were criticized for allowing women the choice to not marry. That did not set well with the Roman patriarchal mindset that held that every woman had to be under the control of a patriarchal figure.

It can be theorized that Christians, attempting to be more socially acceptable to the Romans and to avoid future persecutions, placed restrictions such as requiring marriage for all women, remarriage of widows, not permitting women to have authority or to teach, etc., as limits likely implemented in the name of greater social acceptability. These limits were from then on misinterpreted as Pauline doctrine and passed on to later generations. In reality, on some accounts, those letters restored patriarchal traditions for Christian women—a restoration for which Paul was blamed until well into the period of modern biblical scholarship.

Has this discussion based upon authorship just absolved the real Paul of sexism? That question remains on the table until we look at the passages in 1 Corinthians mentioned earlier. These texts—1 Corinthians 11:2–16 and 1 Corinthians 14:34–35—both found in an authentic Pauline letter, also come into consideration when sexism is attributed to him.

1 Corinthians 11:2–16: On Head Coverings

The issue in 1 Corinthians 11:12–16 is not easily determined, making the passage difficult to understand. One obvious concern is proper attire, especially regarding head coverings, in the Corinthian liturgical assembly. It is not stated whether Paul had received a complaint about this issue, so what triggered his remarks is uncertain.

Paul thinks men should pray or prophesy with uncovered heads and women should be veiled. He embeds this in a patriarchal comment: "But I want you to know that Christ is the head of every man, and a husband the head of his wife, and God the head of Christ" (1 Corinthians 11:3). Paul sees a woman's veil as "a sign of authority on her head" (1 Corinthians 11:10). He also justifies his recommendations about head coverings by referring to the second creation account in Genesis 2:4–25 where the man is created before the woman, then she is created from his rib.

Along with all the remarks in this lengthy passage on male headship and female subordination, including even remarks about hairstyles, Paul seems to nevertheless correct his remarks and return to his usual egalitarianism when he writes: "Woman is not independent of man or man of woman in the Lord. For just as woman came from man, so man is born of woman; but all things are from God" (1 Corinthians 11:11–12). Yet Paul concludes these comments by appearing to try to cut off debate. He says that "if anyone is inclined to be argumentative, we do not have such a custom, nor do the churches of God" (1 Corinthians 11:16). His recommendation that women should be veiled is custom.

Based on this circuitous passage, should we conclude that Paul was patriarchal? Probably yes, at least on some accounts, certainly regarding the social custom of hair covering for women. Notably, what we do not see here is any prohibition of women praying in the assembly. The patriarchal impact of his passage on requiring head coverings for Christian women throughout the centuries has been enormous and remains customary in many parts of the world.

1 Corinthians 14:34–35: The Silencing of Women in the Churches

In addition to the passage just discussed, 1 Corinthians also contains Paul's only other restrictive comments about women in his authentic letters. Finding both of these passages in 1 Corinthians may not be a coincidence. As Paul discusses the exercise of the gift of prophecy in assemblies in 1 Corinthians 14, he offers precise mandates in verses 26–33. None of the directives are gender specific; any member of the assembly, male or female, might prophesy. It is rather unexpected, then, that a statement about restricting women is suddenly made in 1 Corinthians 14:34–35:

> Women should keep silent in the churches, for they are not allowed to speak, but should be subordinate, as even the law says. But if they want to learn anything, they should ask their husbands at home. For it is improper for a woman to speak in the church.

Analysis of the context of these verses reveals that they break up the train of thought in the larger passage. Verses 33 and 36 connect logically and smoothly. Some scholars, therefore, judge verses 34–35 to be a non-Pauline interpolation. If they are correct, the question is to whom they should be attributed: the suggestion is that a manuscript copyist is to blame. That person would have entered vv. 34–35 into the text for personal motives. The interpolation is already in the earliest extant manuscripts so, assuming the theory is correct, the addition must have been done very early. As seen in other instances, this is a case of Paul being used against Paul. His document is forced to favor the silence of women in the churches by someone's later devious work. One could also point out that verses 34–35 are suspicious because they contradict Paul's normal egalitarian praxis. Perhaps the scribe who wished to force Paul's text to silence women was influenced to make the interpolation after copying 1 Corinthians 11:2–16.

In concluding these comments about Paul's attitudes toward women, it is clear that there is no incontrovertible evidence to label him sexist or even a male chauvinist, as some have done. To the contrary, apart from his undoubted patriarchalism over headwear, there are no other grounds upon which to convict him. In fact, he is refreshingly egalitarian in his ancient context.

Do Paul's Letters Indicate He Was Anti-Jewish?

A major question about Paul's thought that takes into consideration all his letters is whether he had become anti-Jewish. It must be emphasized that this is a critical issue since Christianity has had a painful history of anti-Semitism (contributing to the Holocaust) and Paul's writings have been used by scholars, preachers, and teachers to undergird anti-Semitic comments and actions.

As laid out earlier in this brief text, Paul was a lifelong Jew, a Pharisee who believed God had raised Jesus, thus a member of that sect among the many such groups in first-century Judaism called Jewish Christians or Christian Jews. The main reason I emphasized earlier that I, along with most Pauline scholars, feel it is inadequate to describe Paul's experience on the road to Damascus as a conversion is that it implies that he changed religions—which he did not. His belief in the resurrection of Jesus, however, shed new light, or gave him a new lens, as I prefer to describe it, through which to understand his tradition—namely, that Jesus had come as the Messiah with all that that implied theologically.

An essential component of Jewish life in Paul's era was the observance of the law of Moses. The Pharisees taught the many stipulations of the law and observance of the law tended to consume much attention. This is reflected throughout the Gospel stories and in Paul's letters, where he discusses the observance of laws, especially "works of the law" (for example, Romans 3:28). Paul commented in Galatians 1:14 how as a young man he had "progressed in Judaism beyond many of my contemporaries," apparently stressing that he too had become more and more adept or exact in observance of the law (see also Philippians 3:6, where he comments: "in righteousness based on the law I was blameless").

As with observances in many religious traditions, a person can become legalistic, in fact so legalistic that less attention is paid to God and more to keeping laws. Religion, then, becomes like a point system in which a person expects to earn a reward that he or she thinks God owes them—salvation. This redefines a relationship with God as contractual. Both Jesus and Paul resisted letting people fall into this trap.

In Christian scholarship regarding Paul, a significant issue is whether the Judaism of Paul's time preached salvation by keeping laws (justification by works of the law in Paul's terms) and, if so, whether Paul outright rejected his tradition on those grounds. The major Pauline interpreter who has had the most influence in this discussion—until the latter decades of the twentieth century—is the reformer Martin Luther.

In the sixteenth century, Luther focused upon Paul's writings. A biblical scholar and Augustinian priest, Luther became a powerful voice of the Protestant Reformation. At the same time, as a monk, he was frustrated at the legalism in which he felt immersed and at his inability to meticulously observe the rules and regulations of both medieval Catholicism in general and monasticism in particular.

Luther experienced a great spiritual release through grasping Paul's teaching that salvation is by grace, an unmerited gift of God not earned by accumulated good deeds and works of the law. Luther, however, imposed upon his reading of the text the perception that Judaism in Paul's time was as heavily legalistic as was his medieval Christian and monastic culture and that Paul himself had therefore rejected Judaism because of its supposed legalism. Because of Luther's immense influence since the Reformation, that inaccurate perception about Paul has affected Christian interpretation ever since, to the extent that it was long assumed that Paul had become anti-Jewish and, tragically, that Christians should be so as well.

Contemporary Interpretation of Paul and Judaism

In the latter decades of the twentieth century, Pauline scholarship dismantled the position that Paul was anti-Jewish.[4] The most momentous change came in 1977, when the scholar E. P. Sanders published his seminal study, *Paul and Palestinian Judaism: A Comparison of Patterns of Religion*. Sanders demonstrated that, in Judaism, election into the covenant and salvation result solely from God's graciousness and mercy, not from human merit. Regarding law, he characterized Judaism as a life of obedience to God, an expression of witnessing to God one's fundamental desire to remain in the covenant. This resulted in his description of Judaism as a religion of covenantal nomism. *Nomism* means to base conduct on adherence to law, and in the case of Judaism, adherence to the law demonstrates involvement in the covenant.

4. See especially the excellent overview by Maria Pascuzzi, *Paul: Windows on His Thought and His World* (Winona, MN: Anselm Academic, 2014), 138–155.

I have sketched merely the keystone of Sanders' analysis. Suffice it to say that this launched for him and other scholars the task of explaining how—if Judaism is likewise a religion of dependence upon God's grace—does that relate to the salvation offered to all in Christ? Answering that question gave rise to what has come to be called the "New Perspective on Paul," and has been the task of Pauline scholars ever since. The academic literature on Paul of the last fifty years, a review of which is beyond the scope here, reflects much new assessment, leading even to proposals of a "New, New Perspective on Paul." The bottom line is Paul is no longer interpreted as having been anti-Jewish. A new perspective in scholarship has also drawn attention especially to Paul's poignant concern for his people's widespread disbelief in Jesus, a matter to which we will now turn.

What Did Paul Think about Most Jews' Rejection of Jesus as the Messiah?

In Romans 9—11, Paul wrote at length about a question that deeply pained his heart: the rejection of Jesus as Messiah by most of his people, the Jews. He states: "I have great sorrow and constant anguish in my heart. For I could wish that I myself were accursed and separated from Christ for the sake of my brothers, my kin according to the flesh" (9:2–3).

Understanding the sequence of the dense ideas and logic within Romans 9—11 is challenging. Why did Paul launch into these extensive remarks in this letter? On the one hand, the Letter to the Romans is a document in which Paul was laying out his positions on many major theological questions. On the other hand, Paul would have surmised how important this issue was to the Roman Christians since, as reflected in the lengthy list of greetings in Romans 16, they were a group consisting of several house churches, some Jewish and some Gentile. The rejection of Jesus as the Messiah by most Jews must have been a subject of not only frequent conversation, but also consternation.

Paul's wide-ranging thought on the subject reflects his deep struggle for answers. One of his most important sources of inspiration in writing Romans 9—11 was, as elsewhere in his letters, the prophet Isaiah. In his remarks, Paul affirms his love for his own people, God's free election of the people of Israel and choice to show mercy, and the failure of those in Israel who thought righteousness could be attained by works of the law. Their failure was to have "stumbled over the stone [Jesus] that causes stumbling" (Romans 9:32). Paul saw this as predicted by Isaiah 8:14, which Paul phrases in Romans 9:33:

> Behold, I am laying a stone in Zion
> That will make people stumble
> And a rock that will make them fall,
> And whoever believes in him shall not be put to shame.

Paul explains that those who did not stumble—that is, those who understood that righteousness is granted to those who live by faith in Jesus—constitute the remnant of Israel. They are chosen by grace and are imaged as an olive tree, some of whose branches (those who depended upon works of the law) have been broken off.

For Paul, the Gentile believers (who have recognized Jesus as Messiah and understand that righteousness is granted by faith) have been grafted on to the olive tree in their place. But such Gentiles should not boast against the branches: "If you do boast, consider that you do not support the root; the root supports you" (Romans 11:18). Paul explains:

> See, then, the kindness and severity of God: severity toward those who fell [the Jews rejecting Jesus], but God's kindness to you [Gentiles], provided you remain in his kindness; otherwise you too will be cut off. And they also, if they do not remain in unbelief, will be grafted in, for God is able to graft them in again. (Romans 11:22–23)

To Paul, this situation constituted a great mystery. Regarding the unbelieving, he states, "a hardening has come upon Israel in part, until the full number of Gentiles comes in, and thus Israel will be saved" (Romans 11:25).[5] In the end, the result will be "by virtue of the mercy shown to you [Gentiles], they [the Jews] too may receive mercy" (Romans 11:31–32).

Paul and the Empire

Another theme in more recent biblical exegesis is the relationship between Paul and the Roman Empire. Influenced especially by liberation theology and decolonialist approaches in assessments of much literature, scholars have asked: To what extent was Paul, in his letters, for or against the imperialism of the Roman Empire?[6]

Throughout the regions where Paul preached Christianity, the imperial cult, with its exaltation of the empire and its emperors, was vibrant. Architecture, especially including honorific temples and newly erected altars, comprised major symbols of the pervasiveness of both Roman belief and control. For example, just before the birth of Jesus, Herod the Great had erected a temple to Roma and Augustus in his recently completed seaport, obsequiously named Caesarea Maritima, to honor his Roman imperial patron.

The widely publicized concept of the Pax Romana (the Peace of Rome) propagandized the peace and prosperity the Romans had supposedly brought about in their domains. That was despite the fact that their dictatorial rule had been achieved at the end of a sword. By warfare and violence, the Romans subjugated and then massively taxed their subjects.

Often cited as a clear-cut answer to the question of whether Paul was anti-imperial is Romans 13:1–7, which begins: "Let every person be subordinate to the higher authorities, for there is no authority except from God, and those that exist have been established by God" (13:1). Paul continues his admonition with the question: "Do you wish to have no fear of authority? Then do what is good,

5. See the full exposition of this passage in Luke Timothy Johnson, *Constructing Paul: The Canonical Paul*, vol. 1 (Grand Rapids, MI: Eerdmans, 2020), 157–161.

6. See Pascuzzi, especially, 250–275.

and you will receive approval from it; for it is a servant of God for your good" (Romans 13:3–4). Paul wrote this, it should be noted, before the Romans imprisoned him for years. Also, Paul's apparently benign assessment of the imperial government must be contextualized and challenged more broadly.

In 1 Thessalonians 4:11–12, Paul tells believers "to aspire to live a tranquil life, to mind your own affairs and to work with your hands . . . so that you may conduct yourselves properly toward outsiders and not depend on anyone." This advice to live quietly and unassumingly is followed immediately in 1 Thessalonians 4:13—5:11 with one of Paul's most urgent reminders of the Lord's imminent return. In other words, Paul writes that so much is irrelevant because the Lord's coming is near.

Again, as in instances noted earlier, such as his recommendation to be celibate and his attitude toward the social institution of slavery, we see that Paul's apocalypticism trumped many social concerns. He was focused on the impending radically different future with the Lord. The structures of the current world would soon pass away; they were to be tolerated without unnecessary conflict for only a bit longer.

For modern readers who encounter Romans 13:1–7 (a passage not in the lectionary), it is important to note that Paul's apocalyptic context is not ours. For that reason, liberationist and decolonializing perspectives supporting Christian protests of unjust governments must certainly be carefully considered.

While Paul's intense apocalypticism is not ours, and therefore we deal with the world's unjust structures more directly, we should nevertheless remind ourselves that the day of the Lord will come for each person. That encounter will happen; it is our faith.

Chapter 8

Hearing and Proclaiming Paul in the Liturgy and from the Lectionary

The relationship between the Church and the Bible is nowhere more apparent than in the liturgy. Having determined the canon of the Bible, the Church is in turn challenged and inspired in the proclamation of Scripture in the liturgy. Readings from Paul's letters play a major role in this dynamic.

The Second Vatican Council was concerned to increase the biblical literacy of Catholics.[1] This goal was set forth especially in the Council's *Dogmatic Constitution on Divine Revelation,* more frequently known by its Latin title, *Dei verbum*. A series of pastoral recommendations found therein called for preaching to be based upon the biblical texts proclaimed at liturgies. At the same time, a new lectionary structured in the form of a three-year cycle was under development.[2] This schema enlarged the range of biblical texts from both the Old and New Testaments that Catholics were to hear. The lectionary also implemented readings from the Book of Psalms as responses by the worshiping community. This heightened the role of the psalms in the liturgical life of the church. Paul, who regularly quotes the psalms in his correspondence, would have resoundingly approved of this increased emphasis on the psalter.

1. For an excellent overview regarding the biblical recommendations of the Second Vatican Council, see Donald Senior, "Introduction," in José Enrique Aguilar Chiu, et al. (eds.) *The Paulist Biblical Commentary* (Mahwah, NJ: Paulist Press, 2018), xi–xii.

2. For a comprehensive introduction to the lectionary, see Regina A. Boisclair, *The Word of the Lord at Mass: Understanding the Lectionary* (Chicago: Liturgy Training Publications, 2015).

Readings from the Letters of Paul in the Roman Catholic Lectionary

Many Catholics learn about Paul's life and thought mainly through the readings at Mass proclaimed from the lectionary. These excerpts, however, do not comprise the whole of Paul's writings. The principle of selection is often guided by those readings that correspond to the seasons of the liturgical year as well as to feast days.

In the cycle of years A, B, and C, according to which the lectionary arranges biblical texts, selections from Paul's epistles are most frequently heard as the second readings for Sunday Masses. This is true for Ordinary Time, and occasionally for the liturgical seasons of Advent and Lent. Readings from Paul are also found in the lectionary for weekdays. Readings about Paul from Acts constitute some of the first readings in the Easter season during Year C.

Since the selection of readings in the lectionary represents only a part of Paul's entire correspondence, only limited information about Paul and his thought will be gained from the liturgical texts. Much of his writing is never read to the gathered community. To illustrate the extent of Paul's thought a person might encounter in the readings only by attending Mass Sunday after Sunday, I would cite the statistical data compiled by Fr. Felix Just, SJ. His analysis indicates that the lectionary readings for all Sundays, including the solemnities of the Lord and a few other major feasts, represent 31.3 percent of all the verses in Paul's seven authentic letters. Regarding selections taken from the six deutero-Paulines the same listing reflects that 37.3 percent of the verses in those letters are included.[3] In other words, about 69 percent of what Paul wrote and likewise some 62 percent of the writing in the deutero-Pauline letters is never read in the presence of those who learn about Paul only from hearing the lectionary readings at Masses.

3. Felix Just, SJ, "The Lectionary Statistics," The Catholic Lectionary Website, accessed May 29, 2022, https://catholic-resources.org/Lectionary/Statistics.htm.

In his analysis, Fr. Just uses the scholarly approach to the authorship of the letters as was outlined in the previous chapter: Paul is clearly the author of seven letters and his authorship is disputed for six others. While that distinction is standard in Catholic biblical scholarship, the Church itself has not taken a stand on the authorship questions, thus accepting the face value or long-standing attributions of the six deutero-Paulines to Paul. When one opens the lectionary to read a section from 2 Timothy, for example, the lector will see that the reading is introduced as "A reading from the second Letter of Saint Paul to Timothy."

What If I Have Learned That Paul Did Not Write This Letter?

Should a lector who is aware, for example, that Catholic biblical scholars generally evaluate 2 Timothy to be deutero-Pauline—that is, written by a follower imitating Paul—amend the introduction to the lectionary reading? Should the lector omit the reference to Paul and say merely "a reading from the second Letter to Timothy"? The answer to these questions is negative. Although corrective editing out of sexism in the text may seem to be an enlightened course of action, it is not in the purview of the lector. The lector's role is to read what the lectionary has laid out. It is the responsibility of the preacher to explain how contemporary scholarship and theology may disagree with some aspect of a text and how the Church refrains from changing the contents, understanding the texts to be historical material.

This example concerning Pauline authorship, and a lector's surprise that the introduction to the text may not correspond with biblical scholarship, reflects the fruitful situation that has developed in the Church in the past half century. Since the latter decades of the twentieth century, far more Catholics have pursued biblical studies in higher education, in study groups, or on their own. The laity's level of education about the Bible has increased dramatically. This can be traced back to the Second Vatican Council that, among its many concerns, desired that the Church's biblical foundations be taught better to all the faithful. Part of that movement, as noted earlier, was the publication of a new lectionary containing many more biblical readings than people would have been exposed to prior.

Paul's voice, through the pericopes chosen for the lectionary from his letters and the stories about him in Acts, resounds much more through the readings at Mass than it did before the Second Vatican Council. This has, in turn, raised curiosity about this fascinating man and his theological impact. Yes, the lectionary gives us excerpts of his main letters and includes passages containing most of his major ideas but there is so much more rich material to learn about him.

The Lectionary Needs to Be a Work in Progress

Since the Second Vatican Council, the pursuit of Pauline studies has grown significantly. Also, it is notable that many more women have become biblical scholars. These women, along with male scholars who share the same concerns, have brought to their work an acute sense of injustices in both the Church and society regarding race, class, and gender. One ongoing concern has been a strong push to employ more gender-inclusive language in translations, especially with the aim that such translations will be included in the lectionary.[4] At the same time, Catholic biblical scholars have pointed out that the lectionary does not "include many stories of the women who have important roles in the biblical narrative."[5] A number of male figures are also absent. In these lacunae, there is a striking imbalance in the omission of women compared with the men who are not included. This issue needs to be addressed.[6] One stunning example, which effectively constitutes the erasure from liturgical celebrations

4. See Boisclair, 97–98.

5. Bosclair, 98.

6. Bosclair, 99.

of a significant early Christian female leader, is the absence of Phoebe, the deacon of Cenchreae.

The Proclamation of Readings

To read at Mass from a Pauline text, or any biblical passage, is for the lector more than just straightforward reading of a text. Liturgical reading is an act of proclamation of the Good News. Hearing the inspired Word of God announced with conviction is essential for the life of faith of the whole Church. For this reason, proclaiming a Pauline epistle reading requires preparation. Certainly, a lector should go over the text ahead of time and prepare any difficult pronunciations. One also needs to grasp and convey the spirit with which Paul wrote. This requires being conscious of Paul's way of structuring a letter, his line of thought, and his talent for expressing himself rhetorically.

One needs to grasp and convey the spirit with which Paul wrote.

Structure and Rhetoric

As he wrote letters, Paul followed the conventions of his day. The basic format for his letters began with a salutation that indicated the name(s) of the sender(s), the name(s) of the recipients, and a brief greeting. The heart of the greeting was a wish for grace and peace from the Lord Jesus and the Father. Then followed a thanksgiving (such as a prayer), which often anticipates themes to be developed later in the letter. An example is Paul's highlighting of hope in 1 Thessalonians 1:3 and a theme that he addresses four chapters later in 4:13–18. The thanksgiving is found in all of Paul's letters, except for Galatians, a community toward which he passionately expressed his displeasure because they were not following the Gospel he had announced to them.

The main section of the letter, the body, followed next. It indicated the main reason(s) the sender was writing. It often closed with a recommendation or even an order or admonition, then came a conclusion with perhaps a wish for peace, a greeting to those Paul knew, and a blessing.

In discussing Paul's missionary efforts earlier, I noted how he often had much less time to be with his new converts than he wished. Sometimes he would leave a coworker behind to continue teaching the new believers; at other times a member of a community would meet up with Paul and deliver a report about a congregation. Reports often triggered a responsive letter from Paul. He would rejoice at receiving good news, but also get infuriated at the serious problems that occasionally arose either within a church or owing to other missionaries undercutting his preaching, as happened among the Galatians. In response, Paul might admonish the believers but also encourage them, instruct them, and preach to them.

Paul intended his letters to sound as if he were speaking to the recipients. Such writing requires much skill. Just as he might have changed his tone in speech, so he does in the letters. At times he communicates deep affection and gratitude but also, when he felt necessary, anger and chastisement, pleading for change and faithfulness to his teaching.

Nearly every letter of Paul noted a reason to prompt his response concerning some development, crisis, or challenge or, as in the case of Romans, to head off controversies. If we can discern the reason, we can better understand Paul's tone and line of argument. But that is the catch; ancient letter writers communicated differently than we do. While someone today might bluntly state their intention for writing from the start, in Paul's time, the writer would gradually build up to addressing the concern.

Paul's letters also demonstrate that he understood the rhetorical conventions of his time.[7] These rules or customs taught a person how to structure and advance a persuasive argument. They were a major component of education in Paul's era. Whether or not Paul had

7. On Paul and rhetoric, see especially Pascuzzi, 59–62.

been formally schooled in rhetoric is unknown; he certainly made superb use of it. Since he intended his letters to be read aloud, he crafted them as he would a speech in which he advanced arguments to convince his hearers of his position. Various rhetorical devices could accomplish that. For example, Paul employed strong exhortations, reasoned arguments, supportive quotes from the Old Testament, and diatribes in which he set up a straw opponent to argue with him within the text of a letter. He also set up questions that he could then answer. The use of all these rhetorical techniques gives Paul's letters vitality; one senses that he is speaking, even debating, in the room —exactly the aim of his writing. Lectors should plan how to use their voices with somewhat different inflections to mirror the voices Paul portrays and allow their facial expressions to match the intention of the passage.

Paul and the Music of the Liturgy

Paul would rejoice wholeheartedly at the Second Vatican Council's biblical recommendations. He would especially commend efforts to assist modern Catholics to gain a better knowledge of the psalms, texts his letters reveal he knew thoroughly. Colossians 3:16, whether by Paul or one of his followers, summarizes his thought: "Let the word of Christ dwell in you richly, as in all wisdom you teach and admonish one another, singing psalms, hymns, and spiritual songs with gratitude in your hearts to God."

The singing and reciting of psalms were a normal part of Jewish life. Liturgical use of the psalms took place at the sabbath meal and in the temple as well when people traveled to the temple on pilgrimage. Christian assemblies, likewise, used the psalms, as Paul commented in Corinthians 14:26: "When you assemble, one has a psalm, another an instruction, a revelation, a tongue, or an interpretation. Everything should be done for building up."

In a recent conversation about possible Pauline influences in liturgical music today, Steven Van Wye, PHD, noted that music is selected for liturgy that reflects the Scriptures proclaimed in that celebration and the time of the liturgical year. Van Wye, the director of music and organist at Immaculata Catholic Church, San Diego, explained that pride of place is given to singing the words of Scripture and especially the psalms, fulfilling the concerns of the Second Vatican Council. I have no doubt Paul would be pleased!

The Christ Hymn

Scholars have long been fascinated by what appears in Philippians 2:6–11 to be an early Christian hymn, especially because of its short rhythmic (in Greek) lines. It is often referred to as the Christ Hymn. There is no evidence of how the hymn may have functioned liturgically. It may have been composed by Paul or quoted and edited with additions he made to it. Paul introduced the hymn, saying: "Have among yourselves the same attitude that is also yours in Christ Jesus" (Philippians 2:5):

> Who, though he was in the form of God,
> did not regard equality with God
> something to be grasped.
> Rather, he emptied himself
> taking the form of a slave,
> coming in human likeness;
> and found human in appearance,
> he humbled himself,
> becoming obedient to death
> even death on a cross.
> Because of this, God greatly exalted him
> and bestowed on him the name
> that is above every name,
> that at the name of Jesus
> every knee should bend,

of those in heaven and on earth
and under the earth
and every tongue confess that
Jesus Christ is Lord,
to the glory of God the Father.

This beautiful text describes Jesus as kenotic, meaning he emptied himself of his divine status, humbled himself as a human being, and obediently died on the cross. This is the attitude by which Paul lived and which he urged upon believers as he set forth the words of the Christ hymn.

A Final Note

Just as Jesus did, Paul emptied himself, took the form of a joyful, energetic slave of Christ, preached far and wide, suffered greatly along the way, and was obedient, even to death as a martyr. Like his Lord, he humbled himself all to the glory of God the Father.

FURTHER READING

Gillman, Florence M. "1 Thessalonians" in Florence M. Gillman, Mary Ann Beavis and HyeRan Kim-Cragg, *1–2 Thessalonians, Wisdom Commentary* 52. Collegeville, MN: Liturgical Press, 2016.

Gillman, Florence M. *Women Who Knew Paul.* Collegeville, MN: Liturgical Press, 1992.

Pascuzzi, Maria. *Paul: Windows on His Thought and His World.* Winona, MN: Anselm Academic, 2014.

Scholz, Daniel J. *The Pauline Letters: Introducing the New Testament.* Winona, MN: Anselm Academic, 2013.

The Jerome Biblical Commentary for the Twenty-First Century, John J. Collins, et al. (eds.), third fully revised edition. London: Bloomsbury, 2022.

The Paulist Biblical Commentary, José Enrique Aguilar Chiu, et al. (eds.). Mahwah, NJ: Paulist Press, 2018.